My Ow

My Own Directions

A Black Man's Journey in the American Theatre

SHELDON EPPS

To Michele
With Appreciation!
My Best,
Sheldon Epps

McFarland & Company, Inc., Publishers
Jefferson, North Carolina

ISBN (print) 978-1-4766-8858-9
ISBN (ebook) 978-1-4766-4613-8

LIBRARY OF CONGRESS AND BRITISH LIBRARY
CATALOGUING DATA ARE AVAILABLE

Library of Congress Control Number 2022042988

On the cover: The author at his "artistic home,"
the Pasadena Playhouse (photograph by Jim Cox)

Printed in the United States of America

*McFarland & Company, Inc., Publishers
Box 611, Jefferson, North Carolina 28640
www.mcfarlandpub.com*

For my loving family,
St. Paul, Kathryn, Frances and Braxton.
And for LB, who always pushed me
to go further down the road.

Table of Contents

Prologue: Chased by Race

If you are a person of color in America, race is always a factor. Being chased by race is often a terrible reality, and it can sometimes be an advantage. But it is always, ALWAYS a factor in your life. I knew that from a very early age and accepted that as part of my very being. I had no choice. Nor did I want one. I am proud to be a Black man in America, even with all of the challenges, the slurs, the preconceptions and abuses that come along with that designation.

What I also wanted was to be celebrated for my race. That is what I still want, to be celebrated by myself and others for being a Black man in America! A Black artist in America and a Black man in the American Theatre. I have provided myself with that celebration even when there have been attempts for it to be denied by others. I want to be recognized and honored for my race but not to be defined by it, and most certainly never to be constricted or diminished because of what I regard as a wonderful embellishment to my very being. I certainly never wanted to be colorless. God forbid! I wanted the richness of being a man of color to be valued and appreciated. Even glorified! I did not want my race to be seen as a diminishing definition or a limitation. Certainly it never was for me.

This was true from a very early age, as I remember. The fact is that when you grow up in an African American neighborhood, you actually don't walk around thinking about being Black all of the time. Believe it or not, race issues and prejudice are not at the forefront of your thinking ALL of the time. It is simply a part of your existence, much like breathing. You don't necessarily think about it until something makes it difficult for you to breathe. And as we know all too well, that can sadly happen at any moment. But if you have had great support from a loving family and a smart and emotionally well-balanced community, you learn to think about being a person of color as a great advantage. You learn to speak of your race with pride. Also, you very quickly learn that one of your additional burdens in life will be to "represent" your race well. You succeed, if you succeed, not just for yourself but for those who come along with you, and most certainly for those who will follow. And if you fail, that failure may be used as a reason to deny others opportunities. That challenge becomes a heavy one in many ways, but ultimately it can also be a welcome one. Was that burden sometimes difficult to bear? Without a doubt. Were there rewards and satisfactions to be had if one's success pushed doors open and allowed others to move on up a little higher? Absolutely.

Like many men of color of my generation, especially those of us who have had great advantages on our path through life, I always knew that I shouldered that additional burden. The truth is that I have resented it at times and wanted to set down that heavy load. But I knew that I could not. Why? For many, many reasons. First of all, I had that strong family background and that supportive community. I realize that I was very lucky in that way. I was taught to view my racial heritage and my skin color as rich and wonderful parts of who I am. I was encouraged to think that if I worked hard enough I could do anything I wanted to do and be whatever I wanted to be—including president of the United States. Literally! Those words were actually spoken. My parents' generation was never taught to think in such lofty terms, but that was certainly the lesson broadly taught to those of my age. Those born in the middle of the last century when the world and our nation were becoming more highly evolved. Or so we thought. Not so surprisingly for those who felt that way, the truth of that dream of a Black presidency would be tested and miraculously proven with historical impact and incredible grace and brilliance by one who is only a few years younger than me. If I had that ambition at some point, and perhaps I did, I gave up on it. Not because I felt it was impossible but because I moved on to other lofty ambitions.

For me, that was the desire to have a life in the theater, first as an actor and ultimately for the majority of my career as a director. I decided early on that I wanted the world to think of me not as a "Black Director" but as a director who had the good fortune to be Black with all of the skills, the wide-ranging knowledge, the soul and the proven ability that went along with that appellation.

Not a great challenge in the world of the arts, right? One would think that at the time that I was forging my career in the latter decades of the past century that this would not be a problem in the supposedly highly evolved world of the American Theatre which was and is presumed to be more liberal and forward thinking than many other fields. Given that, one makes the assumption that this would not have been a great challenge. One would be wrong! I did achieve that goal. At least among those that allowed that goal to be achievable. There were, and sadly there are, many who do not. At this point I can no longer be worried about them. As the great writer Toni Morrison once said, "I'm tired of it! So I've decided to let racism be the racist's problem, not mine." Those simple words were a great release for me when I heard them, and they allowed this Black man to be defined by his work, his ability, his ambition, and both his failures and his successes, not by the hue of his skin color. That is as it should be.

Blessedly for me it has been that way for many years. Though there are moments that are appalling even now. And most certainly there have been many moments when I have felt the pressure of what James Baldwin and Toni Morrison wisely and poetically identify as "the White Gaze." The additional challenge that comes from the desire to exercise your art, but to exercise it freely, without the necessity of proving to white society that you are good at what you do, according to and frequently judged by white standards. The challenges of building and sustaining a life in the theater are great enough, believe me. Meeting your own high standards and constant desires for growth already requires a great deal of strength and tenacity. It takes years to "knock the little white man" off of your shoulder. To avoid the white gaze and judge your work without looking at it with and through that constantly omnipresent lens. It takes quite a long time to get to the place where you can shut yourself off from that additional obligation. That takes security, experience, probably some success and confidence. It takes a great reliance on knowing what you know! The latter can often be identified as arrogance (and it certainly has been). But believe me, that is far easier to deal with than the judgment and the restricting pressure of that onerous white gaze. That can be the "knee on my neck" that artists of color have been forced to deal with for many decades. We must fight constantly to get rid of it. We must fight to lay that burden down and stand tall.

Sadly, I am writing this at yet another moment of great racial strife in our country, brought about by the brutal and senseless murders of several Black men and women by what seems to be an ever-increasing group of policemen who ignore their pledge "to serve and to protect" in favor of savagely brutalizing people of color to death even as they beg for the simple kindness of being given the breath of life. These recent incidents have ignited "the fire next time" that was predicted decades ago by the brilliant and prescient James Baldwin. That fire is playing itself out in literal and figurative ways with much to be respected and appreciated protest marches, but also sadly with rioting, looting and burning in streets of many major cities all over the country. Indeed, all over the world! I believe that this is not just a reaction to the murder of that good man, George Floyd. His brutal death was the ugly match that lit the bonfire to be sure. But the conflagrations have been fed by years, decades and centuries of injustice and prejudice. Years of inequality in a nation that prides and congratulates itself on believing that there is equality for all. The destruction of that myth is at hand. The cries in the street are demanding acknowledgment, truth and change. And as never before, I think, those cries must be heard.

I do not for a moment pretend or allow myself to believe that the racial injustices that have chased me and burdened me as an artist in America are in any way tantamount to the brutal murders that brought about these protests after years of abuse. But the racial inequities that I have faced have their own brutality and ugliness and have been just as real. They have demanded that I fight back, that I shout, that I scream and that I light my own fires to shine the light on the racism and prejudice that has blocked my road and the roads of so many other artists of color over the years. This moment in time has allowed many to take the breath that is needed to raise their voices in protest and to honestly "call it out," as they say in the Baptist church. It has allowed me and many of my colleagues to call out both the conscious and unconscious racism and prejudice that exist in our field. During this time, I have been asked by many to raise my own voice. Once again. I face those requests—which are both flattering and demanding—with a combination of exhaustion borne of raising my voice over so many years. I force myself to find a renewed energy that comes from believing that this time our voices will be heard.

My story is a unique one and carries some weight both in terms of triumphs and challenges. I have often been one of "the first" or one of "the only." Sadly, during my two decades as artistic director of Pasadena Playhouse, I was always one of only three or four persons of color in a leadership position at a major theater, and for far too many years I was the only one. My hope is that my story can be both inspirational and a cautionary tale, with the ever-burning hope that those who follow may have fewer challenges than I have had, in part because of my journey.

It was a long, hard road to get there. That road had many highs and lows, great triumphs and celebrations. That road also had roadblocks, frustrations and some tears—usually in private. It was a road both bumpy and smooth that took me in many directions. A very long road made both smoother and bumpier by so many aspects of my life.

It is a road that took me in many directions. Most of them were chosen and defined by me. Most of them took me in my own directions....

Making My Playhouse Great

On this long, rewarding journey there was certainly one road that was the most fulfilling and rewarding. It was also frustrating, exhausting and sometimes surprisingly treacherous. It was full of tremendous highs and lows. The journey along that road was all about building a GREAT THEATRE. Sounds like a fairly simple goal, doesn't it? That is what I had in mind when I accepted the job as artistic director of the renowned Pasadena Playhouse in 1997. By that time I had worked on and off Broadway, on the West End in London and at many of the great theaters all over America, including the Guthrie in Minneapolis, Cleveland Playhouse, Crossroads Theatre, and I had the benefit of my four-year stint as associate artistic director at the Old Globe theatre in San Diego. I later would refer to my time there as my graduate school education in what I call "The Art of being an Artistic Director"— and quite a good education it was! And blessedly, I had been watching great theater at many great theaters in this country and all over the world for decades. So I had a pretty clear idea of what makes for theater greatness.

Pasadena Playhouse had many of the essential elements in place when I got this calling: a long and illustrious history, a beautiful physical facility, and the theater is located in greater Los Angeles, a dynamic city with an audience for good theater and an appetite for good work— despite a strong reputation to the contrary. Many of the essentials were in place to achieve this lofty goal. So why not? Surely that's something that could be achieved if I gave it, let's say, a good five-year commitment. So why not? Two decades later, I was still pushing to make this dream a reality with great success, inevitable failures, highs and lows, tremendous rewards and reasons for pride, and most certainly never a week, month or year in which there were not great challenges of all kinds with a scale from hardly noticeable to catastrophic! All of that was in the future. In the moment of decision about beginning this journey I

The historic Pasadena Playhouse, dedicated in 1925 (Pasadena Playhouse Archives).

had the liberty of dreaming of greatness. Any really good artist must of necessity also be a dreamer. So why not let the dream begin?

I did not come to the job strictly as a dreamer or without preparation. I'd had some very good role models who had generously prepared me for the job over the years. Certainly my recent *graduate school training* with Jack O'Brien, artistic director of the Old Globe, had been hugely valuable and informative. But I'd had some great mentors long before that. Going all the way back to my days as a young actor at the Alley Theatre in Houston, when Nina Vance, truly one of the pioneers of the resident theater movement, would come into my dressing room and actually sit not just on, but in the sink and regale me with tales of the early days of establishing her theater. Her stories, told with theatricality and great Southern charms, were both inspiring and often hysterical. I was lucky enough to spend time with one of her compatriots and best friends, the brilliant Zelda Fichandler, founder of Arena Stage in the nation's capital. Zelda was one of the only people I have ever known who could speak extemporaneously in perfect paragraphs—so just imagine how great her prepared and written speeches were. Zelda beguiled me with her own great stories of the founding of the movement. She was especially inspirational when she spoke of "the value" of the work that we do and how it can change our lives and our society. I met the leonine Lloyd Richards, a pioneering man of color in our field (most notably as the director of the first production of *A Raisin in the Sun* and later as partner to August Wilson in the development of his first plays) when he was head of Yale Repertory Theatre and the prestigious Yale School of Drama (now known as the David Geffen School of Drama at Yale). A man of few, but mostly brilliant and profound words, summed up so much for me when he advised me to "Keep your eyes on the prize, not on the prizes." Thanks for that, Lloyd. And in some ways most profoundly, Garland Wright, artistic director of the Guthrie Theater in Minneapolis during one of many shining eras in the history of that prestigious theater. In my brief but very full time there I was able to spend time in "the court of Garland" as it was called, not by him, but rightfully so. This was at a moment in my journey when I started thinking about a life as an artistic director, probably subconsciously. Garland taught me many lessons about being a great one. Patience, trust, faith, staying out of the way until you are needed and then getting into the way (and knowing how to get in the way) when that is necessary. Also knowing that it is not always necessary—that's the faith part. And vitally he subtly taught me about having a vision for a theater that included the artists, the audience and the community and putting equal value on all of those "partners in the endeavor" as he called them. Garland was another fellow Scorpio who inspired me with his brilliant work and his brilliant words, which he was always careful not to characterize as advice. "Just a thought, do with it what you will," he would say about small things or very big ones in his eloquent and dark-hued baritone voice. My sojourn at the Guthrie was brief, but oh so valuable to me. The lessons of these and many other giants in our field truly prepared me to be ready to run the theater. I had a great deal to learn, to be sure. But these icons had given me a real head start and real lessons in how to think about creating a great theater and finding your own way to be an artistic leader. Willingness to dream was a concept that they all shared, which gratefully they passed along to me.

The Pasadena Playhouse was founded in 1917 by another mad dreamer named Gilmor Brown. He came to Pasadena as a traveling player earlier in that century and fell in love with the small but vibrant community's physical beauty, near perfect weather, and his own sense of the potential of the place. He started his theater company in a tiny saloon in what is now called the Old Town area of the city. With great determination, drive, passion and, we are told, a special penchant for charming the "Little Old Ladies from Pasadena," he managed to build a beautiful first-class theater for his company in 1925. This glorious palace of art was in the middle of an orange grove, several blocks from the center of town. Although its beginning was rather humble and certainly much more community theater based (in fact the original name of the theater was Pasadena Community Playhouse), Gilmor managed to push the company into becoming one of the most successful and well-known theaters in the country. It attracted well-known actors and directors and premiered plays by some of the country's most well-known authors. Several years into its life in the magnificent home that he built for the company, he charmed a few more of those little old ladies to build an adjoining five-story building which housed The Playhouse School for the Arts, which for many years was considered one of the best training programs for young actors in the country, helping to launch the careers of Robert Preston, Charles Bronson, Dana Andrews, Sally Struthers, Morgan Freeman and even ZaSu Pitts. Many years later, two of the school's students who trained there were given slim chances for success as actors. That would be Gene Hackman and Dustin Hoffman. A pity that their careers never went anywhere! That misjudgment aside, Gilmor Brown really did accomplish remarkable things at Pasadena Playhouse even before the regional theater movement really took hold in the country.

Alas, one of his few failings was doing little succession planning. When he passed away, no one knew quite how he managed to keep the place afloat and where the bodies were buried (some say literally!). As a result, the theater floundered for a few years after his death, and a bad combination of financial issues, lax artistic standards and the slow diminution of the popularity of the school's training program led to the theater shuttering in 1968. The once beautiful theater was basically gutted by creditors and went into great disrepair. Pictures of the state of the theater during this period suggest that a site-specific production of the musical "Follies" would have been very much at home there without touching a thing! Things got so bad that the theater was nearly torn down in order to, as Joni Mitchell wrote, "Pave paradise and put up a parking lot." Indeed, that exact thing very nearly happened. The building was very much on the verge of being leveled when a few brave souls staged a Norma Rae–like protest to stop the progress of the demolition crew. The efforts of this same passionate group eventually allowed the in-terrible-shape-but-still-standing structure to receive designation for being historically significant. Bulldozers stand down! The theater was here to stay.

Sadly, however, the building did not spring quickly from that brave moment into new theatrical life. The theater was boarded up and remained closed and sadly neglected for many years. There are some terrible photographs of what it looked like as the result of water damage from a leaky roof, lack of maintenance and occasional vandalism. Finally, a gentleman from the real estate development business named David Houk came along and saved the day. Mr. Houk actually had very little interest in the theater or the entertainment business. He was a developer. Based on research, he had come to learn that putting a theater or a performing arts venue at the center of a dicey neighborhood would and often did increase the value of the blocks around the venue. David had a vision of getting the theater reopened, buying up and developing the properties around the theater and populating the neighborhood with new construction of all kinds that would house residential properties, office space, restaurants and retail possibilities. His idea, which was a sound one, never came to fruition during his time at the theater. Ironically, what he had predicted and hoped for (and even drawn up on fully realized plans) was exactly what happened many years later when the theater would indeed be the centerpiece of what became known as a revitalized Playhouse District that gave the city great pride. He didn't get all of that done, alas, but in collaboration with the city, he did rebuild, refresh and reopen the theater and blessedly, based on historical photographs and plans, restored it to its original Spanish palace-style glory. He made some mistakes further down the road, but he should be well credited for that accomplishment. After a few fits and starts, Houk and Associates did get the theater open and functioning once again. And actually it was not long before they were producing with great success and once again being acknowledged as one of the more important of the larger theaters in the Los Angeles area.

I first directed at Pasadena Playhouse in 1991 at the invitation of Paul Lazarus, a longtime friend from my early producing days of running a small (really small) theater in NYC called The Production Company. Paul, during his brief but exciting tenure as artistic director, asked me to direct a good old chestnut of a play called *On Borrowed Time*. It was during the preview period before the opening of that play that I got the call to come down to the Old Globe theatre in San Diego to meet Jack O'Brien to direct a new play called *Mr. Rickey Calls a Meeting*. That phone call eventually led to my graduate school matriculation during my four years at that theater. During that time, I returned almost yearly to direct at Pasadena Playhouse and formed a good association with the current Executive Director Lars Hansen and many on the staff at the theater. Sadly, my friend Paul left the company soon after my first production here. And not long after that Mr. Houk himself exited the building, giving up his adventures in the theater to return to real estate development. Lars Hansen, however, remained and soldiered on, running both the business and the creative operations of the company. Lars was the person who invited me back to direct several times, and we formed a solid working relationship which shortly would lead to an unexpected and life-changing invitation.

Many think that I made the decision to leave the Old Globe because I was offered the position at The Playhouse. That is not quite true. For a number of reasons, I knew that it was time to make a move after working under the auspices of a grant from Theatre Communications Group at the Old Globe. One reason was certainly that both the grant itself and the munificence of a two-year extension on that grant had been exhausted. The theater would have been challenged to maintain a full-time salary for me without that outside support. And I would have been challenged to stay no matter what, given that I had hit a lovely but quite unbreakable glass ceiling at the company. So, I had to "Move On," as Mr. Sonheim would say. After contemplating a renewed life as a gypsy freelance director back on the road once more, dreading the blank, white walls of the guest artists' housing, I had already made the decision to move "up North" to Los Angeles to further pursue a nascent career as a television director, hoping for financial security at last, if not complete artistic fulfillment. When he heard of my plans, I received a blissful invitation from Lars to work with him at Pasadena Playhouse as artistic director on a "half-time basis." A bit of a strange construct, but, as I said, why not? Of course, this was never the case in truth. Especially as my opportunities began to take off in the land of television, which generously supported my theater habit. I found myself in fact having two full-time careers. Challenging, to say the least, but I was young, strong, driven, and perhaps a little bit insane. So, once again, why not?

Over the course of the next many years there were many weeks when I would spend much of the day on the set of a television show and my late afternoons, evenings and weekends at the theater on El Molino Street building the theater! It was challenging, rewarding, sometimes a bit reckless, and quite often exhausting. But somehow I made it work. Both for me and I believe in the theater. My work in the television world fed my work at the theater and in fact directly influenced the growth and expansion of Pasadena Playhouse as I was able to bring artists, donors, and influencers into the life of the theater as the result of my collaborations with many passionate theater lovers who were now finding great success in other areas of entertainment. At a certain point the demands of the theater along with my own slackening energy for keeping all of the balls in the air made this juggling act less possible, and I drifted away from doing television work (before it drifted away from me) in order to fully focus on running the theater.

And focus on the theater I did! I took supportive inspiration from those great men and women who had fought difficult but vitally important battles before me. I asked myself those time-honored and most valuable questions: If not me, then who? If not now, then when? I focused on THIS theater with the vision of building a great theater, as I said. Did I ever actually achieve that goal? That is for others to say. But I do KNOW that we had moments of greatness. Many of them. I do KNOW that it was a far better and more highly respected theater when I stepped down from my position after two decades than it was when I walked into the job with such high hopes and great expectations. I do KNOW that it became a theater that many recognized as first class—a theater to which "Attention must be paid!"

The next two decades of my life would be filled with making this happen, which would make for an often quite glamorous and starry journey. But it started like this....

Shortly after it was announced that I would be ascending to the throne as artistic director of The Playhouse, a very radical weekly newspaper in LA did a feature story praising the decision but predicting that the waters could be much less than smooth. The essay pointed to Pasadena's long history of conservative politics and racial division. The writer expressed a combination of shock and awe that a Black man had been designated to take a leadership position at what was then widely thought to be "a white theater." The article, which made some quite salient points, predicted that my tenure at the theater would not be tolerated by some and might very well be quite short. It predicted that the fair-skinned constituency of the theater would find a way to make a transition in the near future (code for "get rid of me") and take their theater back! The well-written essay was accompanied by a startling and unsettling bit of artwork: an Al Hirschfeld–like drawing of me boiling in a pot of hot oil while wealthy conservative WASP types danced around the cauldron with spears and knives. When I saw the article and the drawing, I was somewhat agitated but also entertained by this aggressive way of depicting my new creative endeavor. When my mother saw it, she merely bowed her head and softly cried. Ever a loving and caring mama! The article, titled "Theater of the Absurd," began with this: "Sheldon Epps may be just the man to bring new flavors to Pasadena, a town known mostly for its vanilla." And later, "Is Epps the man to satisfy the geezers, galvanize the hipsters, placate the board of directors and keep the closet racists at bay? If so, this Black artist leader in a racially complicated community has his work cut out for him." So very true!

There were real reasons for concern. Or at the very least, consternation. The Playhouse was designed in the beautiful and appropriate Southwest mission style and is fronted by a gracious courtyard with a majestic fountain. This commodious space serves as the theater's de facto lobby, given the gracious Southern California weather which offers up balmy days and nights even in the depths of winter. As both a freelance director and then in the early days in my new position, I would frequently sit in that commodious courtyard as the audience gathered before a performance. It was all too often the case that I was the only person under 60 going into the theater

The "Welcome to Pasadena" drawing that made me laugh (sort of) and made my mother cry (illustration by Carol Wyatt, 1997).

and, even more frightening, the only person of any color waiting for the theatrical event to begin. Both things struck me as fundamentally wrong on so many levels. Warning bells went off as I observed this day after day. This represented a great challenge for me and for the theater from the artistic, the emotional and even the business level. A great challenge for every theater in America was an aging audience that might soon disappear if new audiences were not identified and wooed to fill the seats.

The theater community was rife with rumors that this Black guy intended to turn the place into Negro Ensemble Company West and that the existing White audience would soon be running from the theater in droves as I programmed one Black play or musical after another. No one who had paid any attention at all to my career or my vastly wide-ranging taste in material up to this point could have possibly believed that this was true. Nor would it be if I had any business savvy at all. I certainly recognized that the way to shake up this theater and its audience was through the programming. And indeed I did want the support of ALL of the diverse communities in greater Los Angeles. I wanted that both artistically and emotionally. But would it be transformed into an all-Black theater overnight? Not my aim, not my desire, and not my way to the exit door.

But things would indeed change. I believe that any good theater is driven by the taste, passions and artistic desires of its leaders, and that is as it should be. If you don't believe in those qualities in an artistic leader, don't hire that person! Yes, I wanted to produce plays and musicals by artists of color (of all colors by the way), but I also had a well-demonstrated and healthy appetite for Tennessee Williams, Noël Coward, Cole Porter and Shakespeare!

Here's something to remember: One of the great things about growing up as a person of color in America is that you get to know "your own stuff" and your own culture to be sure. But the well-kept secret is that, if one is smart, you also get to know theirs. Either by choice or necessity, you get to know everything about the white folks, but you also get to know everything from your own cultural experience. And that is not often a two-way street. So, being a person of color is in this regard a benefit. I am forced to learn all that you white folks know, and I get to know all that comes out of the Black experience. It is very rare indeed that artists without pigmentation benefit from this equation. I certainly did.

I wanted to make great Art, to be sure. But as the civil rights icon John Lewis used to say, I also wanted to get up every morning to make "Great Trouble." I set out to shake things up in a meaningful and necessary way because it was time for the work on The Playhouse stage and on all of the stages of American theaters to reflect the thrilling diversity, colors and shape of America! So my very first seasons at the theater did indeed include choices from the African American and Latino canon of dramatic literature but mixed in with works by Tom Stoppard, Noël Coward, Moss Hart, David Hare and many others.

These choices were rarely commented on in polite Pasadena society, but there were certainly questions in the air. Would long-term subscribers sit still for such a wide-ranging program, or would they be made uncomfortable by seeing artists of color on the stage and hopefully in increasing numbers in the audience? Would this chase some people out of the theater? Probably. And my firm belief was that it was best to let them go. Running out, I hoped, never to return again if journeying to a world that was different from their own was too much for their delicate sensibilities. Let 'em go!

I firmly believed, and it certainly turned out to be true, that the small number who would go running away would be valuably replaced in much greater numbers by those who would embrace the magic of diversity on the stage and throughout the building.

Did I know that for sure? I did not. Remember that this was well before diversity, "the D Word," became ever so prevalent at major arts institutions. In fact, Pasadena Playhouse was something of a pioneer in this fight. I was taking a chance, yes. But it was more a leap of faith. And one that paid off with rich rewards for the theater in every way. Artistically, culturally, aesthetically, and quite frankly at the box office. Over the next several seasons the shows that rose to the top of the sales charts were those that had appeal to audiences of color. Clearly they were eager to be served up good meals from their own cultures, their own stories and their own experiences. I was happy to do the serving. And even more happy, in fact PROUD to say that this new approach to programming was by and large not only embraced but indeed celebrated by the existing audience at the theater even as it attracted thousands of new theatergoers of all colors into our house. Those "Little Old Ladies from Pasadena" may have been a bit nervous or even shocked at the very beginning, I suspect. But many of them became my most ardent and loyal supporters.

But before any of the highs or any of the lows, before I had a chance to make a theater great, or even try to accomplish that noble goal, there were just questions about how I got there. How did I get myself placed in that cauldron of boiling oil, daring to bring literal and figurative color to an institution which was so proud of its whiteness? How did this man of color dare to ascend to the leadership of this conservative bastion of art and culture in what was one of the most conservative and still racially divided communities in America?

Others asked those questions and other questions that I have often asked myself, to be honest. Over the course of a long and rewarding career, exactly how did I get into so many of "the rooms where it happened" even before I got to Pasadena Playhouse? How did I manage to stand on the stages of Broadway and the West End theaters? How did I manage to travel through my work to so many mysterious and enchanted places, including what they call "The Lots" of Hollywood where I would look up to that famous sign on the side of the hill. As I made my way to and from stages that had been filled years before by the major stars of the stage and screen, and as I shared rehearsal rooms with some of the legends and brightest lights in the entertainment world, there were many moments when it hit me with a kind of blinding reality that creates both tremendous humility and overwhelming gratitude. Somehow I was actually there. But how did that happen? How did I get from the south side of Los Angeles—the "colored" part of town—to all of those rooms and all of those stages? How did I make my way into the executive office of one of the most illustrious theaters in America as its artistic director for two decades? Especially at a time when it was all too rare for a person of color to have such an exalted position? How did I get the chance to work with some of the greatest actors, directors, writers and producers of our time both here in this country and all over the world? How did all of that happen?

As I began my long tenure at Pasadena Playhouse and set out to make it a great theater, those questions lingered in the air, in the press and, to be quite honest, even in my own mind. How did all of this happen? After all, I was just a kid from Compton....

ACT II, SCENE ONE

Making My Way to the Stage

That was me. Just a kid from Compton. In truth, that IS me. A "PK" from Compton in fact. A preacher's kid. My father, a wonderful preacher whose spiritual fervor and love of language inspired my later artistic life, had been sent to Southern California in the late 1940s by the higher-ups of the Presbyterian Church to start the first Black congregation of that denomination west of the Mississippi River. It was from watching my father, St. Paul Epps (and yes, that is his real given name), that I learned about leadership, community building, and most certainly the persuasive use of words and language that would become both a lifelong passion and a frequently effective tool for my work in the theater.

Beginning this long and eventful journey as a kid born in Compton Hospital in the early 1950s is quite meaningful. Though at that time it was a "Negro Community" that one might say was on the upper edge of the lower end of things economically speaking, it is still quite remarkable that the road started there and led to Broadway, some of the greatest of the great American theaters and major venues around the world. Even (somewhat surprisingly) success in Hollywood as a television director of some of the most iconic series ever produced. In all of those areas, I was often "the first" or one of "the only." That was a source of pride, a burden, an obligation and a blessing—often all of those things at the same time!

What makes this so surprising is that there were many, MANY, who did not get out, who did not escape these either humble or, at the very least, challenging beginnings. Years later, when I returned to the neighborhood, I looked around and saw men of my age hanging around liquor stores in varying states of malfunction brought on by whatever substance abuse was their burden. I would look at them with both compassion and consternation. Were they schoolmates who had traveled no further than a few blocks from our nearby homes? Why so short, limited and clearly challenged a road for them and such a long, rewarding, unexpectedly fulsome and sometimes dazzling road for me? Luck? Good fortune? Parenting? Determination? Perhaps a bit of talent? In truth, the latter means nothing, or can mean very little if the other variables are not in place. And in a bigger truth, there is no real answer for why me and not them, other than it is simply what Fate and the Universe devised for each of us as we made our journeys in this particular lifetime.

Those humble beginnings in Compton were not without some very rich rewards. Certainly not of the monetary kind, but very rich rewards, nonetheless. That was the result of a childhood during which I enjoyed

So handsome ... even at a very young age. Circa 1958.

the tremendous love and support of a great family and an even greater community. So what was in reflection a somewhat poor life on a preacher's salary was in fact very rich in so many other ways.

In truth, I don't think that our family was ever actually poor. It's probably more accurate to say that we were "fiscally challenged." Honestly, I did not feel it at the time and only became aware that this was indeed our economic condition many years later when my mother would talk about how far she sometimes had to stretch a pound of ground beef or what a luxury it was when we had a weekend treat of hamburgers and hotdogs at a food stand in Watts, which along with my older siblings, my sister Frances and my brother Braxton, we all looked forward to as if it was Saturday night at the Ritz. Though even that much anticipated fast-food delight was a step ahead of the previous generation, at least on my father's side of the family. He used to say that for years he thought that the only edible part of a cow was the gravy! But perhaps I did not feel the level of our modest life because of the richness of our community.

The mission that my father established, quite deliberately named Bel-Vue Community Church, was indeed very much at the center of this community. The church held its first Sunday service in the garage of our family's home at 118th St and Avalon Boulevard. In due time, through my father's diligent work and the loving support of my mother, a beautiful mission-style church was built half a block away on an empty lot that was large enough to later be expanded to include a community center and education building which housed a variety of activities including Boy and Girl Scout troops, Bible study classes, baking sales, youth orchestra rehearsals and Sunday social events after the morning service, to name just a few. St. Paul believed that the church should be kept active and alive as often as possible and not just on Sundays. I heard him say once that he wanted to serve the soul but also the hearts and minds of those in the community of every age. As his congregation grew and evolved, this became very much a reality. To this day I meet people here and there who tell me that the Reverend Epps and Bel-Vue were integral and vital factors in their growth and give full credit to my father and this rich community for pushing them to higher levels of achievement in their personal lives and their relationships. Given the number of times that people have said to me, "Your father married me and my husband" or "Your father kept me out of jail," I sometimes wonder how he had time to work on his Sunday sermon! But somehow he did, and often gloriously so.

Befitting his designation as a Presbyterian minister, not a Holy Roller or even a Baptist, those sermons were not full of hellfire and damnation, but they were rich in spiritual fervor, inspiration, linguistic eloquence, literary references and true contact with his God. I suppose I did not really pay much attention to his admirable execution of his own art form as a young child. I'm sure that I was as squirmy and eager to get out of Sunday services as any eight or nine year old. But at some point I wised up, and I began to marvel at his ability to move people with his words and the fervor with which he delivered powerful sermons each and every Sunday morning. Many years later, when I had truly come to appreciate this great oratorical gift of his and when I was conscious enough of the idiosyncratic brilliance of his craft, I asked him

how he made that possible. He said to me, simply but movingly, "Well....
I get up every Sunday morning and have a talk with The Lord. He helps
me to think of something that will set my soul on fire. Then I go up into
the pulpit, and I let them watch me burn!" Needless to say, I sat in profound awe of such an incredible answer for several minutes. Such a powerful lesson. And one which I readily admit stealing for my later work. I
have frequently delivered those words to a company of actors on opening night. "Set yourselves on fire, and let us watch you burn." This simple but inspiring theatrical lesson from St. Paul has helped to lift many
an opening performance to much higher ground.

Another thing that provided me with my rich upbringing, whatever the actual economics of our existence, was the fact that both of
my parents were admirers
of the performing arts.
They both believed that
it was vital for all of the
young people in the
church community to be
exposed to the arts at an
early age. In order to
practice what he literally
preached, my father and
mother saw to it that we
all had constant opportu-
nities to be exposed to a
variety of cultural expe-
riences, including sym-
phony concerts, dance
recitals and even opera,
both within the church
and at various perform-
ing arts venues all over
Southern California.
And, oh so lucky for me,
on one or two occasions
this included theater performances as well.

So it was that early
on a Saturday or perhaps

My lovely sister and me "performing" in Los
Angeles, circa 1960.

a Sunday morning I found myself, along with several others from the church, boarding a bus to take a long ride to a theater on the other side of Los Angeles to see this thing called a play. It may very well have been the first fully professional performance I had ever seen. I probably had no idea what we were going to see as those choices were made by others. But after leaving the bus, I learned quickly from a sign outside of the theater that the afternoon's entertainment was going to be something called *The Member of the Wedding* by Carson McCullers. Looking at the poster, I realized that the name above the title was one that I actually recognized, Ethel Waters. I'd seen Miss Waters on television variety shows, primarily as a singer. I certainly had no knowledge of the fact that this was a play in which she had enjoyed tremendous success on Broadway and at many other theaters over many years. I suspect that she was giving one of her final performances in the play at the matinee that I saw, as she was quite old by then. But her theatrical star power was still very much alive and on display and could be felt even in the upper reaches of the balcony where I sat that day, leaning forward towards the stage.

Two things hit me that afternoon. As the leading role in the play is the character of Frankie, a teenager struggling with identity, self-esteem and finding "a place to be" in the world, I suddenly dis-

My stylish mother, Kathryn, my father and me after a church service at Bel-Vue, circa 1960.

covered that those things called plays could actually be about me and have relevance to my own life. I was just at an age where I was dealing with similar issues of my own, so I was engaged emotionally in the theater for perhaps the first time in my life. Engaged, moved and enlightened! On that afternoon, I discovered the theater's power to reach in and touch the soul in a powerful and unexpected way. I learned that a play could have both questions and answers that related to my own life and my own experience. That a play could "hold the mirror up" to my own nature and reflect my own youthful yet complex challenges as I was soon to enter my turbulent teenage years.

The second thing that I discovered that day was the definition of the word DIVA. Thanks to Miss Waters, I had a true education that afternoon in the art of star power! Yes, by then this great actress had played the role many times, and I suspect that her effects were finely calibrated and perfected, both in all of her scenes and her soulful rendition of the song "His Eye Is on the Sparrow." She took this spiritual and turned it into the equivalent of an aria full of depths of soul and spirituality that I had never before experienced. Somehow, even with all of the technique in the world in place, Miss Waters managed to add the elusive elements of heart and humanity to her performance, which she shared with the audience in ways which were subtle yet gargantuan and ineffable. I'm sure that I had seen magicians by that time in my life, but I certainly had never seen anyone create MAGIC on the stage in the way that she did that afternoon. Her performance was justifiably rewarded with one of the most inventive, stunning and well-deserved curtain calls that I had seen before or since! Nobody took a bow like the great Ethel Waters!

Now all of this would probably make for a better story if I could tell you that it was on this day that I decided to have a life in the theater. Wouldn't that be lovely? But I cannot claim that this is true. I was committed at that point to a career as a lawyer. Odd to say that I was committed, as I probably had no idea what that meant, but I would maintain that particular career goal for many years. Actually from quite an early age until right before graduating from high school. But it was on this day that I fell in love with going to the theater, and I have participated in that rewarding habit throughout my entire life. Unforeseen circumstances would soon give me the opportunity to exercise this newfound thrill in quite a substantial way. More anon on that! From that time on I was always hoping to be as moved as I was that day by the power of a story acted out before me, by the power of personal identification with characters on the stage, and with the hope that I would see the same kind of presence and star power that Miss Waters offered up so generously that day. There is no doubt that this special afternoon at the theater changed my life!

Here is the part of the story that people always think I made up to give this tale a bit more heft or an extra level of appropriate drama. However it is a boldfaced truth that the theater where I had this epiphany and fell in love with the art of the theater was The Pasadena Playhouse. I would in a few years walk through the courtyard and into that theater many, many more times. For many years on an almost daily basis. I found my artistic home very early in my life.

But it would be many years before I visited that theater once again. Shortly after this first visit to The Playhouse my family made a rather "dramatic" move across the country. My father's grand and glorious achievements at Bel-Vue Community Church brought him much attention both locally and nationally. As a result he was asked to join the administration of the Presbyterian Church, which was housed at the Interchurch Center in NYC, several blocks from Columbia University and across the street from Grant's Tomb. I got to know both of those venerable institutions quite well on days when I would visit my father in the gleaming office building that some called the Protestant Vatican on the Hudson. His new job took all of us to a strange new land on the other side of the country.

Act II, Scene Two

From Coast to Coast

This cross-country move meant quite an upheaval for me and for my family. Towards the end of my first junior high school year I was suddenly transported from the safety and comfort of my hometown existence to an exotic place called Teaneck, New Jersey. This was the suburb across the river where my parents had purchased a new family home from which my father would commute to his new office position in Manhattan. For all of us, this was a big move in so many ways—physically, emotionally and even economically. My father had been given an engagement bonus by the church hierarchy which allowed him to make a down payment on the house in New Jersey. I suspect that the salary in his new position was quite a bit higher than that of a neighborhood preacher which he'd been receiving for so many years. I think that I was able to figure that out because suddenly we were eating out at better restaurants and there was less discussion about what we could or could not order based on the menu prices. Within reason. The furrow on my father's brow did tell us that some things were even now off limits.

I'm sure that I did not know the meaning of the word myopic at that time of my life, but myopically speaking the move was just a lot bigger for me than it was for anyone else in the family. I felt very strongly that I had moved not just from one coast to the other, from one city under the California sunshine to a bleakly gray town in New Jersey, but from one civilization to another with all kinds of changes that literally rocked my world.

Let me explain why this transcontinental transition was quite so traumatic for the kid from Compton. In Los Angeles, I had enjoyed the comfort and safety of my father's church congregation and also the warm embrace of a nearly all-Black community. It wasn't that we never saw White people. We did, of course, in the media and also in exchanges "across town" when we would go to the fancier shopping areas, to performances or to restaurants on the other side of town. But the truth was that my day-to-day existence was by and large entirely in the warm comfort of an African American community including neighbors, schoolmates, friends, doctors and teachers who were all Black. As this had been the case since the day of my birth, this was the color of the world that I knew, and I felt safe, warm and comfortable in that world. I was rarely if ever "the one" in any situation that I encountered. That was about to change!

Teaneck, New Jersey, may as well have been a foreign country. In the mid–1960s this small town was already a mixed community, but not one that was truly integrated. There was a clear line that defined the areas where Black and a few Latino people lived very much separated from the predominantly Jewish community that represented a clear majority of the township's population. I guess I had been a smart kid back home in LA, with a pretty outstanding scholastic record (so good in fact that I actually skipped a full grade). So, given the "tracking system" that was in place at Ben Franklin Junior High School, I was the rare Black child who was deemed to be smart enough for placement in the upper-level classes. As a result of that decision, and certainly through no choice of my own, when I started classes shortly after our family's move, I shockingly discovered that I was the only face of color in almost all of my classes in my new school. I was indeed suddenly a stranger in an even stranger land. One Black face in a disturbing and uncomfortable sea of Whiteness. And I was in no way prepared to swim in these unfamiliar waters.

The further complication was that many of those pale-faced cherubs around me were members of the Jewish faith, something that I knew little about and did not comprehend at all. I was confused and confounded by new words, new holidays, new culinary possibilities (What's a bagel?) and even new pieces of clothing. What could possibly be the reason that the boys had to wear those tiny little caps that I came to understand was something called a yarmulke? Certainly that thin, round material could not be used to keep their heads warm. These new classmates were far too young to be covering even very premature bald spots. As I said, I was very clearly confused and confounded by it all! My parents tried their best to be supportive and understanding. But there was little that they could do to help me as I walked through these new classrooms and hallways in a dazed state, feeling a bit like an alien on a strange planet. Add to that the pressure of being covertly stared at whenever the word "Negro" was mentioned in history or social studies class. That term was now not only a designation but actually one of the people in the room. Oy! I had no idea what that term meant yet, but most assuredly those two letters aptly described how I felt.

This mental and emotional miasma quickly had me talking myself into every possible physical ailment that I could imagine. Headaches, nausea and upset stomachs. I would even have tried gout if that would have helped me to avoid going to school. It did not take very long for St. Paul and Kathryn to suss out that none of these illnesses were real, but merely manufactured to keep me away from school and this strange new world as often as I could get away with it. However, as a child who had blessedly always been very healthy and not at all prone to any of the maladies which I now claimed (especially the gout), I did not get away with it for very long. After a visit to a new doctor who pretty much verified my parents' opinion that it was all in my head, they had a firm but loving talk with me and let me know that I would need to find other ways to deal with my new situation than coming up with the "illness du jour." It was a much-needed time for tough love. And that is exactly what they gave me as they reminded me that I was capable, smart and strong enough to meet the challenges which they acknowledged as real. It was both their sensitive understanding of the difficulties of this period of adjustment and their always present encouragement and belief in my ability to both overcome and rise above it all that got me through this very tough period and allowed me to "keep on pushing." Their support gave new meaning to a song I heard often in my father's church and allowed me to believe that "We Shall Overcome." I very much needed that assurance at the time.

Somehow I settled in and pushed ahead and at least accepted this new not so normal without perhaps fully relaxing into the new reality. This east coast situation was still very odd, and the many cultural and societal differences that had been thrust upon me would remain challenging for quite a while. In remembrance I now recognize this transition as one of the most difficult and challenging times of my life. This was truly a turbulent period that was jarring to me physically, mentally and emotionally. However, in some ways, this difficult bend in the road also led me to the beginning of a journey which would define my entire life. I often wonder what my life would have been like if I had remained in Compton and never moved with my family to the east coast. I was not to know then and I certainly do not know now because the journey that I have taken is the one that I was meant to take.

There was a very cherished upside of this dynamic geographical change. The location of that upside was the magic kingdom that I quickly came to learn was just a few miles away from Teaneck, New Jersey. If you drove due east and crossed the Hudson River by way of the George Washington Bridge, you entered that wondrous place called New York City! Mine was not the story of a country bumpkin who came to the Big Apple from some small Southern or Midwestern town. Up until this time I'd lived in the very sunny city of Los Angeles, which was no hamlet. But truly I was not prepared for the majesty, the dazzle and the excitement of Manhattan. Even more splendiferous was the true magic that I discovered there in an area of the city that I quickly came to love and that I embraced immediately. The traumatic cross-country move that my family had made enabled me to get to a very special place. A place called Broadway.

ACT II, SCENE THREE

Magic Time

My mother and I developed a very special and very close relationship during the months and years after our cross-country move. We had always been close and loving but became even more so during this time. My father's new position required him to travel around the country on business for the church, so he was frequently out of town. My sister Frances was in college by then in Knoxville, Tennessee, and my brother Braxton was doing whatever teenage boys do, which meant that he was frequently MIA around our home. That meant that my mother and I spent a great deal of time alone together after school and at dinnertime and quite frequently over weekends when my father was on the road. I always knew that she enjoyed the performing arts, but during our life on the West Coast, I never really thought of her as a theater lover. Quite happily, with Broadway theaters just across the river now, I was about to learn that she was. And lucky me, I got to be her theatergoing buddy for many a matinee beginning in the spring of 1964 when we moved to the other side of the country. At that time theater tickets in the upper reaches of the balcony were relatively inexpensive and not nearly the luxury item that they have become. So, for around $20 the two of us could afford the bus fare into the city, two balcony seats and even lunch together on a weekend afternoon. Truly!

And so it was that I found myself climbing with her up to the second balcony of the beautiful St. James Theatre on West 44th Street on what I believe to be the first of these Saturday excursions to see something called *Hello, Dolly!* I probably knew a little about the show because the recording of the title song by Louis Armstrong had become a major hit and was played on the radio quite frequently. I am sure that I must have seen Satchmo belting it out on the popular television variety shows during that time. I suppose I suspected that perhaps I would see him live onstage at the St. James. That did not happen, of course. But by no means was I disappointed. Because on that afternoon I was transported for the first of many times to "musical comedy Heaven."

I would later learn much more about the names of people like Gower Champion, Jerry Herman, Carol Channing and David Merrick. In fact, through one circumstance or another I actually met all of that illustrious group and worked with some of them. All I knew on that day, however, from my quick perusal of the title page of the Playbill was that those people and a whole lot of others had come together to create this magical "thing" called a musical that unfolded in front of me.

From the moment the lights went down, I was enraptured by the sound of the orchestra, the dazzling colors on the stage, the evocative charm of something that I later would come to know as choreography (brilliantly created by Mr. Champion), and swept away by the much bigger-than-life, but still somehow completely believable, behavior of Miss Channing and company. I would later hear and come to understand the term "pulse quickening." Certainly that was not something that I would have said at that moment, but equally certainly it was something that I felt as a result of the power of what emanated from the stage. A stage that was charged with enough theatrical electricity to touch my heart and soul even in the upper reaches of the St. James balcony. And believe me, that is quite a reach! From these seats in the second mezzanine the people on the stage were actually quite tiny. But the theatricality was BIG and bold! I remember that what I experienced that day was that there was a physical power that came from the creation of JOY on the stage. It was not just what I saw and what I heard, but what I felt! Including the indescribable feeling that this joy was being shared between everyone on the stage and the thousand other people in the theater at that particular performance. It certainly began when that train to Yonkers came out on the stage as everyone was putting on their Sunday clothes (and yes, I discovered that you could actually sing about that and have it make sense). That feeling continued on through the next hour or so and built to a peak by the time Miss Channing came down those stairs in that famous red dress and was greeted by that immaculately tailored group of waiters as they welcomed Dolly back home again. Suddenly we were all in it together, all transported to the Harmonia Gardens to celebrate this momentous occasion, all surrounded and immersed in the pure JOY of the theatrical moment!

I would eventually learn that this kind of power in the theater can be created in any number of ways and that it can ignite every conceivable human passion from dark to light and tragic to celebratory. I felt a tinge of it certainly about this just a few months earlier back in California when Ethel Waters sang that beautiful spiritual seemingly just for me. But on that day I discovered it in the very distinct and special way that can be delivered by masters of the craft working at the peak of their game to create that magical thing called "A Broadway Musical." I would learn to love this form even more in years to come. And I would learn to love so many other theatrical forms equally as well. I would feel that power in theaters large and small over and over again with the work of other musical masters over the next five decades as well as in the genius of the Greeks, Shakespeare, Noël Coward, August Wilson, Tom Stoppard, Lynn Nottage, Twyla Tharp, Duke Ellington, Cole Porter, Stephen Sondheim, Hal Prince, Bob Fosse, Michael Bennett, Lloyd Richards and so many others. But on this special day it was all about that woman in the red dress who traveled down to NYC from Yonkers to bring herself back to life before some parade passes by. We were all on the journey with her, and we all shared the joy of her journey. It was quite a lesson!

I took to going to the theater like a baby who has just discovered mother's milk. I would still travel over the river and through the town frequently with my mother, but I soon found the gumption to make this trip on my own. Very quickly going to see Broadway shows became my weekend activity. No football games for me. I would scrape together the bus fare and enough dollar bills for many more balcony seats. And after a particularly frugal week, I might even have the extra dollar and a few cents for an Orange Julius (remember those?) freshly blended for me at the stands actually on Broadway. How glamorous was that?!?! I know that this was only possible because the price of the tickets was unimaginably low. For some reason the figure $4.25 seems to stick in my head. I suspect that it may have been a bit higher sometimes and perhaps a little lower occasionally. Stunning to think of that now. So this was doable, but only if I gave up other things to save what I could of my small, weekly allowance or cafeteria lunch money, which I was happy to do! When even that amazingly low ticket price was out of reach, I learned the art of "second acting," sneaking in to see shows at intermission, grabbing a Playbill and searching for the section where hopefully I could find an empty seat. This latter activity was particularly useful for returning to see a show that I had already seen in its entirety. I laugh now as I remember myself lingering across the street from many a theater until act one came down, and the doors would fling open for patrons to come outside, usually to smoke at that time. I would then make a carefully calculated nonchalant move to the sidewalk in front of the theater, mingle with the crowd for a moment or two and then boldly slip inside and scope out where the empty seats were, or perhaps a place at the back of the theater in the standing room section. Now and then you would get a raised eyebrow, a stern glance and even rarely a verbal rebuke. But certainly not often enough to discourage me from continuing to exercise this act of rebellion, larceny or exuberance. Over the next few years I would see all of hundreds of shows and the second act of dozens of others!

As I remember back to my theatergoing habits in those early days, I did tend towards seeing many musicals. But somehow this crazy kid would frequently be attracted to a vast variety of theatrical styles. I became enamored of the pages in the *NY Times* Arts and Leisure section, which on Sundays carried the huge display ads for upcoming shows in the season. Many of the names that I discovered there I certainly knew from television and LPs (remember those?). But many other names were literally foreign to me. But I would make my way to those theaters for any number of reasons. Sometimes I thought that the artwork for the show looked interesting. Or there was a name, like Noël Coward, that I had heard but knew nothing about. And, of course, there were titles of the great American plays that I knew from literature classes that I wanted to know not just from the printed page but as they were intended to be seen … on the stage. As a result, I saw not only a huge number of musicals—both good and bad—but also a vast variety of plays, including the work of Arthur Miller, Tennessee Williams, Edward Albee, the aforementioned Coward and even Molière. Go figure! There were probably many afternoons when I left the balcony not really sure if I understood what I had just seen but never regretting that I'd pulled together the six dollars that I needed for a ticket, bus fare and a hotdog or hamburger, usually at the counter of a Howard Johnson's restaurant that was on the corner of 46th and Broadway. Good or bad, play or musical, big stars or unknown names who I came to know well over the years, it did not matter. For me, each of those afternoons up in the balcony was blissful!

Now, I should mention that I clearly had the blindness of innocence during these jaunts into New York City and obviously the blind faith of my parents as well. As many will remember and as some do not know, the theater district was a far different kind of place during those years, prior to the massive cleanups of 42nd Street and beyond that took place once the Disney Company came in and bought and restored the New Amsterdam Theatre as a home for their stage productions. This was the era when that street was called "The Deuce" and that the area surrounding the theater district had far less glamour than it does now. Hard as it may be to believe given the current healthy state of the Broadway industry, at that time it was not at all unusual for me to pass several theaters that were without a tenant and many that were shut down seemingly for long periods of time judging by the signage on them with the cheery advice, "Go See a Broadway Show," when they had none on offer at that moment nor for several months before or in the future. It is probably an exaggeration to say that you took your life in your hands to get to a Broadway show at that time. But it was a dicey experience. Either I didn't really know that, or I simply ignored any real or imagined danger as I blithely headed from the Port Authority Bus Terminal towards whatever theater was the point of my destination for that day. I do believe that I was smart enough to avoid ever actually walking down 42nd Street, which even in my innocence I recognized as having no relationship to the cheery venue described in the well-known song from that eponymous musical. Even the naïve, youthful me was smart enough to know that the feet on that avenue at that time were doing things other than dancing and that the denizens during this period were rarely described as nifties! Instead, I cheerily headed up 8th Avenue and waited to reach 44th Street. There I crossed over, heading towards 7th Avenue and Broadway, and usually cut through Shubert Alley to take in the posters for whatever shows were running. Turning that corner was a little like Dorothy opening the cabin door and discovering the Land of Oz in all of its glorious color. So what if I had to pass a few Show Worlds with their peep shows and perhaps run into a weary hooker or two to reach that theatrical alley. It was well worth it for what awaited me once the curtain went up in those palaces of art, which in truth were somewhat shabby at that time. But I never noticed, I am sure. And somehow, it never even occurred to me to be scared by what I later learned was a dangerous neighborhood. I just felt safe, at home and very excited to be going to the theater!

There was a very special thrill that went even above and beyond the overall exhilaration that I got from my afternoons in the theater. That was when I saw a show with a predominantly Black cast. One of the first was *Golden Boy* starring Sammy Davis, Jr. I was a huge admirer of his from television variety shows, of course, but nothing was quite as special as seeing him live on stage. I remember his tremendous presence, his versatility, charm, expressive vocals, and a thrilling choreographed boxing match that was the "eleven o'clock number" of the show. This was the kind of term that I was learning to know well. Sammy and his opponent threw themselves into this incredibly realistic fight that was choreographed down to the fingertips, I am sure, with abandon and tremendous skill. It was heightened by a propulsive musical underscoring and percussive hits which gave me some understanding even then of how a naturalistic scene could be theatricalized to tremendous effect.

I also remember the charm, vivacity, star quality and beautiful vocals of Leslie Uggams in *Hallelujah, Baby!* Not a very good show overall, then or now, even with countless revisions. But it did have a wonderful musical score and terrific performances by the entire cast and Miss Uggams. As I watched, bedazzled by her beauty and charm, it certainly never occurred to me that I would not only meet her one day but actually work with her several times and become a close friend of this divine creature who made my teenage heart flutter.

One of the most special afternoons was spent once again at the St. James Theatre with that famous Dolly girl. This was a few years after that first epiphanic encounter with the show. I returned to see it after David Merrick, the producer, had the sly and ultimately hugely successful idea to reinvent the show after it had been running for many years on Broadway by bringing in an entirely new company of Black actors with the dynamic duo of Pearl Bailey and Cab Calloway in the leads. If my heart and head swelled with excitement the first time I saw the show, and they did, then they must have come close to exploding when I saw this incarnation. Somehow, beyond the obvious reality of the complexions of the company, everything seemed more colorful. Everything seemed more musical and even more joyful. Both the kicks and high notes somehow seemed even higher. Mr. Calloway brought his own incredible energy and verve to the role of Horace (including interpolations of his famous and iconic scat singing and Minnie the Moocher dance steps). And then there was Pearl. Her Dolly was Thornton Wilder's, Jerry Herman's, Gower Champion's and somehow completely Pearl's all at once. She brought to the role the same humor, charm and vivacity of previous Dollys but added her own indescribable finesse and quite profound soulfulness to the role in a way that made her Dolly simply soar off of the stage. The ovation that she received when she walked out for her curtain call in that white finale dress, which so beautifully set off her dark brown complexion, was the one of the most overwhelming that I had ever seen. Once again, as Miss Waters did back at Pasadena Playhouse, Miss Bailey defined the term "star turn" for me that afternoon. Needless to say, I saw the second act of that version of the show several times!

As I said, I was pretty blissful almost every time I went to the theater. But there was something profoundly special at this point in my life in seeing those productions which featured a Black company of actors, including shows such as *The Wiz*, *Hallelujah, Baby!* and *Purlie* (which ironically I would direct twice decades later). This was at an era when despite many advances, racial equality was still a great issue for people of color, when the most basic human rights were being denied—an affliction which sadly and unbelievably carries on today. But on Broadway I was able to see performers with dark skin at the very top of the game. Denying the validity of racial prejudice with the strength and beauty of their skill and ability. With their very presence. Whatever issues they had once, they left the theater, and I am sure there were many, they truly reigned supreme during their time on the stage and declared themselves with a kind of pride, dignity, spirit and expertise which was hugely meaningful to me at that time in my life. These shows definitely elucidated a popular phrase of the time because they were filled with their very special Black Power!

Even in my nascent understanding of all things theatrical, I knew that Broadway was the top of the game. And here were all of these beautiful Black and Brown faces owning the stage without question and with tremendous authority. I was encouraged once again to believe by watching them that "We" could do anything! The lessons that had been given to me from my very early years by my parents, relatives and churchgoing community were completely validated by my getting to see these shows specifically. I received this much-needed education with an open heart, and I carried their divine inspiration with me then and well into my own future.

Those afternoons up in the balconies of Broadway theaters were truly Magic Time for me. In the midst of the usual teenage angst that I was facing, exacerbated by the sudden move east to a new society and culture, I found in going to the theater something that simply gave me joy and happiness. In the last rows of those theaters I was transported to all kinds of magical places, told remarkable stories through words and music; I was made to laugh and sometimes cry but always left those buildings somehow feeling better about my life and about myself. That's a kind of magic, isn't it? I thought so then, and I still do. The theater can have a healing power and most certainly can give us all kinds of reasons to feel JOY. I was soon to discover that I also had the ability to weave that magic. Quite unexpectedly I was soon experiencing the magic of the theater not just from the balcony but on the other side of the footlights as well.

Getting Stage Struck

The young girl named Frankie in the play *The Member of the Wedding* states at one point that she is "Looking for the we of me." For me the attraction to actually doing plays, as well as going to see them, was very much attached to this goal. I was also looking for "the we of me" much more than I was contemplating any visions or dreams of making a life in the theater. I still had aspirations of being a trial lawyer during my early junior high school years (though I suspect I don't really know what that meant). I suppose it bears noting that this profession has its own inherent drama, so maybe I was not as far away from theatrical ambitions as I thought I was. But certainly I was, like Frankie, looking for and in fact needing a community, a place to be, after our move to New Jersey. Though not often alone, I did feel quite lonely. I lived in the Black neighborhood, but I was the only face of color in almost all of my classes, so making new friends did not come easily as I was a bit betwixt and between academically and socially. I was a small kid, and sports had never been of much interest to me, so I did not drift towards the football or soccer teams that might have been an after-school activity. I think that it was the love of language that I inherited from my father and a curiosity about what actually went into making a play that had me drift towards the drama club. In that group of slightly nerdy and certainly offbeat kids I found a community that welcomed me and which I welcomed. I felt at home with this oddball group who found great fun in spending an hour or two "putting it together" to make short plays and skits which we then performed at school assemblies for our classmates. Once you reached ninth grade you got the great honor of fully rehearsing a full-length play and performing it in front of an audience over a weekend of performances.

Thornton Wilder's American classic *Our Town* was the work chosen in the year that I was first eligible to participate in the spring play. Wilder's great play was and is enormously popular at all levels of production.

It is as American as you can get, both funny and emotionally moving, and it has lots of good parts. The latter being a particularly important factor for a school production. Other than wanting to continue to hang around with my drama club buddies I have no idea how or why I got the notion to actually audition for the show. Lord knows I knew very little about this play, Thornton Wilder, and absolutely nothing about the art of acting. Previously, to participate in the assembly one acts, all you had to do was show up to be guaranteed a role. But an audition was required for this one. I don't think that I even understood what that meant. But I think that the drama club sponsor and the director of the play, Mr. Cowen, patiently explained to the group that attended the orientation meeting exactly what he wanted to see. Following his instructions carefully, I showed up the following week with my three-minute monologue prepared along with everyone else. Somehow I landed on King Arthur's monologue from the musical *Camelot*, explaining how he became king by pulling the sword from the stone. How I landed on this particular speech, I know not! But I remember that I found the book in the school library in the drama section, learned the monologue and did my thing for Mr. Cowen and my schoolmates on the big audition day. Perhaps it was an early predilection for fairy tales and myths that led me to this choice; I'm not really sure. But somehow, preparing it on my own with no direction and no coaching at all, it went pretty well. I remember my classmates applauding when I finished, which was quite a shock. I think that a good part of their reaction came from acknowledging the audacity of this little "Negro boy" somehow finding the chutzpah (one of my newly discovered words) to actually play King Arthur. Yet somehow to me it seemed perfectly natural. Mr. Cowen asked me to stay after everyone else departed. I suspected that he was going to tell me that I did OK but that there was not really a spot for me in the show. After all, the play was about white people in Grover's Corners, New Hampshire. I was prepared for the worst and ready to accept my fate as an assistant stage manager or a spot on the prop crew. Instead he told me that he was "blown away" by my audition and that he was going to have to rethink his casting choices based on my unexpected audacity and shockingly good audition. Way to swell a ninth grader's head!

A few days later we sat in the school auditorium once again as Mr. Cowen announced his decisions about who would be in the play. Not surprisingly for a drama teacher, he built suspense by starting with the smaller roles and saving the larger ones for last. Finally he got to the plum role of the Stage Manager and said that the part would be played by ... not me! Then, after the shortest but longest of pauses, he said, "Oh, I forgot one thing. I never expected that this would happen, but because Sheldon did such a great audition, he will also play the Stage Manager for two of our four performances."

Did I really hear that? Could that really be true? Well, I guess I did, and I guess it was, as shortly after the meeting broke up, everyone came over to congratulate me and to celebrate this good news. I suspect that I was a bit in shock as I thought about playing the leading role in my first full production of a play. Pretty mind blowing. Even if it was only for two performances!

I will be quite honest and tell you that I don't remember very much about the whole experience during rehearsals and for those two performances. Having seen the play many times since then, I am sure that I had little to no idea what it was all about at the time. But I did learn the lines and the blocking, and I was probably just as good and as bad as any 13-year-old boy has ever or could ever be playing this role. Many years later I saw the great Henry Fonda playing the stage manager quite brilliantly in a Broadway revival. That experience made it clear that I certainly had missed nearly everything that was available in this great part, but who knew that at the time? Again, it would be great to tell you that it was this experience that made me decide to spend my life in the theater and that from that time on I knew that a career on the stage was what I wanted. Once again, that would be a better story. But ... that is not the case. It was just a good experience with some like-minded schoolmates that kept me happily busy for several weeks after school. A fun time that gave me the community that I had been searching for, that gave me that much-desired "we of me." Not life changing nor career defining. But there was something about it that gave me comfort, warmed my soul, and made me want to participate more in this thing called playmaking.

And so, the theater became all consuming in some ways. Between after-school rehearsals during the week as I went into my high school years and my still ongoing jaunts into the city to see Broadway shows on the weekends, I found myself "in the theater" for many hours every week. And best of all, I no longer gave myself morning maladies to stay home from school. Indeed, I was happy to go. The end of the school day now meant meeting up with my community of friends to go to "play practice." Suddenly getting through the day was just fine, in fact easy, as I had that to look forward to.

Over the next few years, as I started attending the very grown-up Teaneck High School (the one public high school in the town), I kept luxuriating myself in the joys of playmaking with my newfound community. Usually the school produced a play during the fall semester and a musical in late spring. Fortunately for me, a kind gentleman named Mr. Reilly, an art teacher and the director of the musical, started working with the Parks and Recreation Department to also keep things going with a production that rehearsed over summer break and did a few performances in late July or early August. It was through all of these activities that I ended up doing parts in such plays and musicals as *Dark of the Moon*, *The Boyfriend*, *The King and I*, *Finian's Rainbow*, and even to land the plumb role of Mordred in *Camelot*, the musical that gave me my start with that monologue that got me cast in *Our Town*—way, way back in ninth grade! How time flies....

As a result of all of these productions, I started to get a bit of a reputation as one of the "dramats" at the school and to either be praised or scorned for being in that particular group. I believe that it was probably in my junior year that I suddenly stopped thinking of this as a hobby or an after-school activity and began to lean into the idea of actually making a go of a career as an actor in the theater.

Two pretty monumental life events pushed this forward. Both took place during my senior year at dear old Teaneck High, which was grandly described given its architecture and a slight rise in the road as "The Castle on the Hill." One would bring me to a heady highlight of my high school years, and the other would lead me to the course of my life through my college years and for much of my early career. Both of them came about as the result of a dare.

Anticipation built quite early among us dramats and others when it was announced early on in my senior year that the spring musical was going to be *My Fair Lady*. I'm not sure that many of us had seen the show onstage, but most of us had certainly seen the wonderful screen version of the show. Those of us who paid attention to such things knew that it had a great score, beautiful production elements and, most important of all, really great parts! By this time I was beginning to develop a bit of an artist's ego and was hubristic enough, crazy enough, or just plain stage struck enough to say out loud to those few who listened that I really wanted to play Henry Higgins. Where the hell did I ever get THAT idea into my little colored boy head? But I did. And as auditions approached and we started talking about what role we were going to audition for,

I mentioned this lofty ambition and was told by another in our little group, "That's crazy. But go ahead. I dare you!" with the clear implication behind the threat that it wouldn't, couldn't and should not happen. That, of course, was enough to get my triple Scorpio ego ignited and all fired up. The director of the show this year was an English and literature teacher, Mr. Brancato, a dark-haired, handsome man whose Italian roots showed in his dramatically Lothario-like good looks! No one of any gender or sexual persuasion could fail to recognize that this man was damned good looking. Dramatically so! When I told him that I intended to read for this part, one of the best and most challenging in the canon of musical theater, I was fully expecting a kind but generous suggestion that I might think about making another choice—Doolittle's sidekick, for example. I was somewhat surprised and taken aback when he stared at me for a moment with his dark, mischievous and challenging eyes and simply said, "Go ahead." His response held only permission, but little promise and even less encouragement. But he also did not say, "Never gonna happen!" So I forged ahead. I learned one of the Henry Higgins songs and prepared a scene or two with one of the girls reading for Eliza. We went in on the day of the auditions, did our thing. I thought it went pretty well, but all we got from Mr. Brancato at the end of the reading was a nondescript, "Nice." Once again, not terribly encouraging. I suddenly started to resign myself to a spot in the chorus or perhaps as one of those backup buskers who sang behind Doolittle and tried to get him to the church on time with a little bit of luck! I'd have the usual fun and good time I was sure, but secretly I was already a bit disappointed.

A few days later, a notice went up that everyone who had auditioned should meet in the school auditorium at the end of the day. We all gathered with Dickensian great expectations. I was by this time completely sure that I was fated for the ensemble and resigned myself to looking good in those Ascot Gavotte costumes. Disappointed but not unhappy with my fate. (Well, not too unhappy.)

At the start of the meeting Mr. Brancato announced that he would be posting the ensemble smaller part assignments later that day or in the morning. He happily and proudly told us that there had been so many good auditions that he had decided to double cast all of the leading roles and that each person would play two of the four performances. Seemed fair, and also a strong validation of how many very talented kids there were in our school at the time. He then went through all of the principal roles, ending with an announcement of the two young ladies who would share the role of Eliza: Jill and Sally. As we applauded that choice, he suddenly started to pack up his valise as if he were about to leave. We sat there with confusion in the air and question marks in thought bubbles over our heads. Once again, quite dramatically, he suddenly came back to the group and said in a quite offhanded manner, "Oh, I forgot one thing. For all four performances the part of Henry Higgins will be played by Sheldon Epps." A stunned moment of silence from me and everyone else before my generous classmates burst into enthusiastic applause and cheers. Mr. Brancato turned to me and gave me a mischievous wink very quickly as I sat there both thrilled and immediately daunted by the task ahead of me, simultaneously excited and regretful that I had taken up that dare.

Now remember, this was long before the days of nontraditional casting. Nobody had thought of the term, the subject or the concept at that time. I suppose that the practice was widely in play in most academic situations. And yet there seemed something monumental, groundbreaking and momentous in his choice to have this little Negro boy endeavor to stand in the shoes of Rex Harrison and take on one of the most challenging and ambitious roles in the entire catalogue of musical theater—remember that the book of the show is based on a Shaw play, that most of the dialogue, at Mr. Harrison's insistence, comes directly from *Pygmalion*, the original source material. What made him think that I could do it. What made him think that I was the ONLY one in our class who could do it, given his choice to double cast all of the other parts? And most of all, what made me think I could do it? And why did I want to? Frankly, I don't think that I thought deeply about any of those questions at the time. I just knew that he wildly, boldly and somewhat wickedly gave me this opportunity, that I wanted to do the part desperately, and even with that combination of ego, hubris and passion for the theater that I described, I knew that I could be good in the role.

And believe it or not, I really was good! I worked really hard on the part, probably leaning a bit too heavily on the Broadway cast recording and Rex Harrison's iconic and distinctive delivery of the songs. But who wouldn't? Especially at that age. Something told me after a couple of weeks to stop listening to Mr. Harrison and make it my own. And, amazingly, I did.

Now and then I have had moments in my life when situations have encouraged me to strongly believe in past lives and bringing things into your current existence that make you more capable in certain areas that you have any right to be. That is why I believe that some people are incredibly gifted with skills in music, art or languages at an early age, well before they have any specific training or any reason to be so advanced in those skills. This was the first time that I was encouraged to believe that something in my own past life had prepared me to understand and to use language well. I would have the same feelings a few years later when I suddenly took to the work of Shakespeare with a deep understanding and an apparent facility for speaking those words with ease when there was nothing in my background in this particular lifetime which prepared me for a kinship with The Bard. I felt like I was Henry Higgins and that those words belonged to me! Excuse me, Mr. Rex Harrison, this was my part! I owned it. At least for those four performances. And somehow, madly, crazily and magically I did own it and gave a performance that got me my first standing ovation, a phenomenon that would be remembered by classmates when I encountered them YEARS later. How gratifying it was to have someone come up to me at our 20th high school reunion and say, "Yeah, I remember you in *My Fair Lady*. You were great. I'm so glad you're still working in the theater. I knew you would." I suspect that I probably was not quite that great. But how nice that somebody thought I was. How nice that it was a performance that was remembered even decades later. Though I am sure those memories were amplified and heightened by the mist of memory. Was I good in the part? Yes, I admit that I was. Was I great? Probably not. But nice to be remembered that way. Very nice indeed.

By that time I knew that I was going to study acting in college. Among many other gifts (including finding my first real girlfriend in Jill, one of my two Elizas, and for a while my very own fair lady—how romantic), playing this role was a great parting gift from Teaneck High before I headed off into the world ahead of me. But let me go back a bit to the other pivotal event that informed where exactly I would be studying drama and actually learning something about acting a few months later. Another pivotal moment when I responded to a dare. Clearly that was a big thing in my senior year!

By the time we reached 12th grade, there was a small group of the larger group of "dramats" who had really determined innocently and madly that we wanted to make a career of working in the theater. Although a late bloomer to that choice, as I finally gave up my aspirations for a future as a lawyer, I was one of that small group. Either in late summer or right at the start of my senior high school year, I informed my parents of this desire and my intention to try to have a career as an actor. I remember a combination of hopeful pride and abject fear and concern that clearly projected from their loving faces at that moment. But their support for my desires was as strong as it had always been. "If that's what you want, that's what you should do," they declared. "But ... You MUST go to college!" No moving across the river to New York City, studying at the American Academy of Dramatic Arts or HB Studios for me. I had to go to college and get a degree. The phrase "something to fall back on" came up several times, as I remember. Meaning that with a degree and perhaps later training in another area, I could at the very least get a teaching job if the "acting thing" did not work out. I was persuaded both by their logic and by the knowledge that a college education was a requirement for young Black people in those days. Certainly for young Black people in my immediate and extended family. All of my cousins had college degrees, many of them achieving this as the first in their family as their parents were farmers and laborers. The value of a college education was something that was drummed into each of us and to all of us over many years. And so, I accepted this fate calmly and actually with little or no teenage rebellion. I also knew by then that there were good schools that would validly prepare you for a professional theater career. I did further research and applied to several of them.

I believe that it was shortly after the Christmas holidays when several of us young thespians who had made the passionate but perhaps insane decision to apply to colleges to study our chosen art form were sitting around in the school cafeteria, discussing the schools that we were pursuing. Many of the usual names came up. Northwestern, Syracuse University, NYU, probably UCLA and Yale, of course. At some point someone mentioned Carnegie Tech (soon to be known to me as Carnegie Mellon University). I knew little or nothing about Carnegie, which prompted the highly intelligent question, "What's that?" I believe that the full-of-himself young man who brought up this odd-sounding name scoffed and said, "You don't know about Carnegie? It's only the oldest and the best drama school in the country." I bowed my head a bit in embarrassment as he continued, saying, "You should apply, but you will never get in. In fact, I dare you to apply!" There was something slightly challenging and more than a little bit racist in the throwing down of this gauntlet. That, of course, got my blood running hot! My head lifted, my heart pounded and I made my way to the school library that afternoon to research this odd-sounding place in a strange land called Pittsburgh, Pennsylvania. My research told me that Mr. Pompous was correct in one aspect. Carnegie Tech did indeed have one of the oldest professional training programs offering a drama degree in the country. I quickly recognized several names of well-known and highly respected actors who had studied there. Shortly after that I discovered that admission was on the basis of an audition process. A highly selective audition process, I was told. It seemed that they traveled all over the country for these tryouts, and I learned that of the hundreds who auditioned every year, the school only accepted a total of 40 in the acting option. Highly competitive, indeed. Hence, the dare from Mr. Pompous! But somehow, once again, that combination of young ego, hubris, and perhaps complete ignorance and innocence kicked in, and I quickly got off an application just before the deadline to apply. Just a few weeks later, I found myself in a Manhattan hotel conference room in front of a rather intimidating and motley group of teachers from the school including the Department Head Earle Gister. I did my two monologues and left, thinking that my chances were slim but feeling proud because I had met the challenge. Dare me, will you? Watch out! I actually suspected that this is as far as it would go with the ratio of 500-to-600 young people auditioning for the cherished 40 slots to be filled by actors from all over the country. Whatever, I told myself, somewhat protectively. There were other good schools. I knew that I would get in somewhere.... Wouldn't I?

About a month later acceptance letters started to come through the mail. I was admitted to a couple of the choices that were high on my list and felt good about that. But I was disappointed that I did not hear anything from Carnegie. Not even a "thanks, but no thanks" letter. Just around the time that I had pretty happily set my sights on another school, one of those extremely fateful but very slim envelopes that can be momentous was waiting for me when I came home from school. The letter was so slim in fact that I immediately assumed it was a letter of rejection. So I opened it rather slowly, staving off the bruised ego, only to discover that it was a brief but heavenly choir letter telling me that I had been admitted to Carnegie. Hallelujah, Baby!

School Daze

Off to school in Pittsburgh! Perhaps that should have been my strong affirmation. But my true thoughts were off to What and Where? Because, by taking that dare several months earlier, I had actually gotten myself into what I soon learned was a highly exalted situation without all that much knowledge about what was ahead of me. Either in that strangely named city, at that highly competitive school, or what the path was going to be for the rest of my life. It was all to come into focus rather quickly because just a few months later I packed a traveling trunk and headed to Pittsburgh to begin the next chapter of my life at Carnegie Mellon University.

Though many have considered me then and now to be a rather cautious person and quite deliberate and circumspect, the truth is that I am a bit of a thrill seeker. I love amusement park rides, parasailing, sliding down waterfalls and hanging off the sides of hot air balloons. The more the danger, the bigger the thrill, the more exciting and attracted I am to the experience. Up to a point, I suppose. I confess that this is still true and clearly was at this time in my life. I should also mention that I was about to be a very, VERY young freshman in college in a very complicated training program. I started elementary school early because my birthday was quickly approaching early in the school year. I also skipped a grade before we moved to the east coast. So I actually graduated from high school and started my freshman year at Carnegie at the young age of 16! A very well-kept secret by the way, as I did not want to explain why that was true, and this was certainly not a distinction that I wanted as one of the 40 in my class.

That exalted-but-soon-to-be-humbled 40 out of the hundreds that started that year with me. I'm sure that we arrived at our new home believing that we were at the top of the heap. We were cured of that undeserved notion very quickly.

The academic legend is that every new class of actors would be gathered in one of the department's two theaters, either the main stage or the studio space, and instructed in this way: "Look to your right. Now, look to your left. Here's the truth. Only one of you will be graduating from this program." Gulp! I don't remember those words ever actually being spoken to our class, though those in upper classes swore that they always were intoned in the first week. Whether they were verbalized or not, I do remember that you were either encouraged or allowed to believe that those words were true. Not only were you not all that special; you were actually rather expendable. And two out of three of you would be gone before the diplomas were handed out or the caps were tossed at graduation ceremonies four years from now. As I said, Gulp!

The pressure of this knowledge was intensified by what we soon learned would be an incredibly rigorous schedule. The day would begin each and every day at 9 a.m. with a class called Dynamics, which was a combination of yoga and relaxation stretches followed by a vocal warm-up. This lovely early morning session, attendance required, was followed by a full day of classes covering all of the required tools for our noble profession: six to eight hours every day of acting, voice, speech and movement classes with a bit of theater history and dramatic literature tossed in. We had only one elective class, and that was usually focused either on studying music or the history of painting and sculpture. More Art! In those first couple of years, a short break for dinner was followed by scene study rehearsals and the joys of "Crewing," which was a fancy term for the cheap labor that we did as production assistants building and painting sets, constructing costumes, and serving on the run crew for the productions in the theaters that would be showcases for the upper-class actors. How we all longed to get to junior and senior year so that those evening hours would at long last be taken up with rehearsals for plays that we would actually be in! Discovering that this was to be our schedule and the days of our lives immediately and seemingly forever made it very clear very quickly why it was probable that only one of three would survive this rigorous life for more than a year or two. We only had ourselves to blame as we all passionately wanted to be one of the elite 40 in the program. Be careful what you ask for!

The next four years (or at least three of the next four years) would prove to be exciting, adventurous, thrilling and eye-opening in so many ways. They would also be exhausting, frustrating, anger making, terrifying and sometimes soul destroying. The combination of such a rigorous schedule, the pressure of having to be "invited back" at the end of every year—hence the winnowing down of the original 40—and the discovery by some that a life in the theater was just not what they wanted took quite a toll on my schoolmates. My particular class was hit by all of this even harder than most and hit very quickly. Within a very few weeks, we would show up for the blissful early morning Dynamics session to find out that someone had departed. This happened with increasing frequency during our freshman and sophomore years, and our class was cut by more than half at the end of our second year. Several others did not receive the coveted invitation to return after that brutal year, and there were a few who graduated early as they had credits which made it a three- rather than a four-year program for those lucky few. The combined result of this mass exodus meant that by the time we reached our senior year, the predicted formula had been surpassed, and there were only seven of us left. This, of course, gave our "Gang of 7" a certain amount of power and arrogance and more than a bit of a rebellious streak. This was most dramatically demonstrated about halfway through our final year.

Because of an illness of a faculty member, we were suddenly assigned a guest teacher who in a short amount of time gained a terrible reputation for cruelty and abuse during his work with "the underlings," our poor friends in their freshman and sophomore years. Earle Gister, the department head, decided that it might be good for us to experience a little humility under his tutelage and filled the vacant faculty

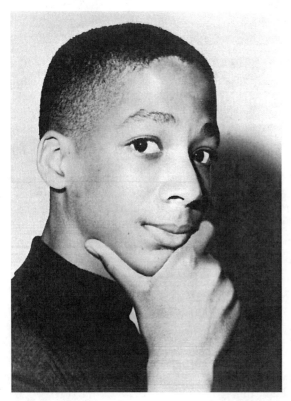

My first acting resume photograph in 1972. Very dramatic.

spot with this gentleman, who, as I recall, was from a small Eastern European country. Or at least he pretended to be. He began the first half hour of his first class with us by berating us in a nonstop, heavily accented monologue, telling us that we had learned nothing about acting at all, that our work was shit, and that our true training would begin that day! He finished that hectoring with his first command to us: "Now take off your clothes and get down on the floor." Little did he know that we had heard those same words far-too-many times over our first three and a half years and that we were oh so weary of stripping down and being stripped down in the name of good training. So that first command turned out to be his last. As instructed many years before, we looked to our right and looked to our left. Only this time it was to get silent but unanimous agreement on our next action. With no words spoken at all, we stood up jointly and headed out of the classroom as he screamed at us in an odd combination of English and Eastern European curse words. We pressed on and left not only his classroom but the entire Fine Arts building and crossed the campus, landing at the student center. Quite calmly we settled in over coffee and waited for whatever would be next. It was not long before dear Earle came running in, clearly out of breath from a swift trot across the campus. "What happened?" he breathlessly intoned. We looked back calmly and said with no confrontation in our joint voice, "No thanks, Earle, not for us. Throw us all out if you like, but we will not be taking classes with that man." Earle took a breath, intending to deliver words of authority and command, I am sure. But seeing the strength in our eyes and our unified sense of resolution, by the time that breath reached his vocal chords, the word that came out was "Okay." And he left. We had a new teacher at our next session, and this theatrical coup was never discussed again. The power of 7!

Our behavior that day was brazen to say the least, perhaps even foolhardy. But we knew that having made it that far, we were in a position to ask for respect and less abusive treatment. That kind of defiance would become much more commonplace in years to come, but at that time it was almost unheard of. But we had a secret weapon in our pockets. We knew that they had to graduate somebody that year, and as long as we presented a united front, they were never gonna throw us all out! So we won! I suspect that we became an even more headstrong, hubristic and overly confident gang of seven who had a pretty easy time of this final year knowing that we all would have good parts, no danger of being asked to leave and as smooth a path to graduation day as any senior class had experienced before or since.

Even though it was quite the roller-coaster ride, I have great appreciation for my days, months and years at CMU. It was a long, tough road. But the thing to be appreciated and celebrated is that the training was as good as it gets in the academic situation. That very special faculty taught us well and prepared us for the careers ahead of us. I often said that you could summarize the training in this way: in your first two years you had "acting problems" to be criticized, challenged and overcome. In your last two years you had "special qualities," those things that were distinctive about your personality that made you special and that would help you to work. In many cases those things were exactly the same, and those deep problems became assets to be refined in preparation for trying to get a job in the real world after you left the security of this dramatic chicken coop. This formula was a bit crazy but effective in many ways. I suspect that in the end, if you were lucky, it did in fact rid you of issues that needed to be addressed in all of your work and then wisely bolstered you for the tough world we were about to face. We were encouraged to think of ourselves as the crème de la crème as Miss Jean Brodie would say. I am sure we weren't all of that. But it did give us confidence and a strong sense of ourselves as artists in those last few years. Beginning to think of yourself as an artist was valuable, as it provided a kind of strength that would be sorely needed as we hit the next leg of our journey. For me, that next leg would begin even before graduation day.

The Real World

The more than slightly cocky attitude that my small but mighty graduating class had during our senior year began to shift very quickly as the ice melted in Pittsburgh and we realized that the sweet smell of spring in the air also meant that graduation day would soon be coming. While we were no doubt eager to be "sprung" from our four long years of intense training, it also meant that we would be leaving the safety nest of dear old CMU where roles were guaranteed and bills were paid either by gracious parents, scholarships, student loans or some combination of all of the above. What lay just beyond graduation was the real world of auditioning, trying to make a living, going from being on the top of the heap as an elite member of the small graduating class at one of the best training programs in the world to being just another actor making the rounds and "waiting for that one big chance to be in a show." That reality seeped in slowly but surely and balanced our upper-class arrogance with a well-disguised but quite palpable fear.

One elusive but encouraging possibility came through the auspices of a great organization called Theatre Communications Group, commonly known as TCG. This was the premier service organization for a huge number of the major resident theater companies all across the nation. Shortly after the Christmas break, we started to talk with faculty members and amongst ourselves about something called TCG auditions seriously and often. This was one of the many great opportunities that the organization provided at that time (sadly no longer available) that served young actors and the member organizations well. These auditions provided a huge opportunity for those students graduating from the best of the professional training programs. The casting directors at TCG held preliminary auditions all over the country and would see all of the members of the graduating class of these schools and then make selections of those who would go on to the final auditions held in Chicago, which would be attended by representatives of dozens of the major theaters around the country. A pretty tremendous way to get your face, body and your talent in front of artistic staff members from all of the theaters that we'd talked about over the four years of our time at CMU. We heard stories about members of the classes before us who were lucky enough to make it to the final auditions, and that opportunity resulted in actual employment at such illustrious theaters as ACT in San Francisco, Arena Stage in Washington, DC, the Guthrie Theater in Minneapolis and many others. We also knew that the percentages were small. We understood that a very lucky few of our previous classmates had made it through the whole process and had actually found jobs. There were far more stories that drifted back to the Fine Arts building about those who were now in NYC or Los Angeles waiting tables and working in offices between all-too-rare auditions. Or—and this was the worst possibility—tales of those who simply could not face the fact that graduation from Carnegie was not the golden ticket that they hoped it would be, so they swiftly left the business completely. That was both frightening and heartbreaking.

So a good deal of time in the second half of senior year was spent on preparing for TCG auditions. In fact, as I remember, the majority of our acting class time in this home stretch was devoted to finding material, trying it out and landing on the choice of the two monologues (one contemporary and one classical) that we would present in the preliminary auditions in late March, hoping to be one of the "chosen few" who would then go on to Chicago a few weeks later. We faced the possibility of getting one of those precious slots with a combination of high hopes, prayer and probably a bit of abject despair and terror.

Some combination of talent, tenacity, uniqueness and tremendous luck got me through those prelim auditions and landed me one of the coveted slots as a finalist for the auditions in Chicago. I am sure that early diversity efforts were also at play in this, as a well-trained Black actor graduating from one of the most respected schools was something that theaters were just beginning to appreciate and value.

Then and now, timing means everything. I did my audition turn in the Windy City on that eventful day, along with about 40 other actors from nationally recognized schools whose names I knew well. At the time I only knew the name of one other person there, the talented young lady from my class who had also been chosen to attend. But years later I found the roster of those who had auditioned on that fateful day and was both amused and impressed to see names on the list that I came to know well over the intervening years. Indeed there were several that I would later work with on various projects both in theater and television.

The day was broken up into two parts: the auditions in the morning and then a round of meetings with reps of the attending theaters that afternoon ... IF you were lucky enough that anyone actually wanted to talk to you! I prayed to be invited to at least a meeting or two. And gratefully I was! Even better than that, at one of my meetings I was asked to return after the end of the session to sing for the representatives of the illustrious Alley Theatre in Houston (certainly one of the places that we had dreamed about working). It turned out that they were actually trying to cast the young male role in their upcoming production of *Jacques Is Alive and Well and Living in Paris*. This was a show, though quite popular, that I knew nothing about, and I knew even less about Monsieur Brel. They sent me off with the sheet music for one of the songs. I pleaded at the front desk of the hotel where the meetings took place and a kindly desk clerk allowed me to sneak into one of their ballrooms with a piano, where I plunked out the melody of the song enough to make some kind of attempt at it when I met with the folks from the Alley a couple of hours later. I sang a cappella the song from the show and one of my audition songs that I'd also prepared in anticipation of life in the demanding real world. I suspect that both were probably horrible, but the people from the theater were either tone deaf, very kind, or in the forefront of those previously mentioned diversity efforts. They allowed me to leave the room believing that maybe it had not been the worst thing they had ever heard.

During that same day, I had meetings with a couple of other theaters that asked me to stay in touch and one that promised to be in touch as they came to a clearer idea of what they would be doing in the upcoming season, with a promise that they hoped "something right would be available." I went back to school the next week, happy to know that there was hope in the world but also knowing that I could just as easily be on the audition path in NYC or working at one of those restaurant jobs in just a couple of months. Things could be worse.... I'm not sure how, but I told myself that things could be worse.

There are a few times in my life that have prompted me to feel profoundly the strength of that beautiful line from *A Streetcar Named Desire* intoned by Blanche at one of the few moments of hope that she experiences in the play. "Sometimes there is God.... So quickly." One of those moments would occur in the week after I returned from Chicago.

I was back in school and in early morning Dynamics once again (yes, even in senior year!). I saw the Drama Department Head Earle Gister approaching me breathlessly for the second time that year. This time with a kind of energy that was a combination of boyish excitement and paternal pride. He told me to get dressed and come to the office with him because the Alley Theatre had just called his office to say that they wanted to make me an offer to do the show and to come to Houston right away. In this "so quickly" moment, I remember Earle eagerly and generously scribbling down the long-distance code that I could use to call them back from his office. I called. Happily I was on a plane to Houston, Texas, about four days later to start rehearsals the next week.

After a quick drive back home to New Jersey (yes, I did have a car in my senior year, thank you very much—a very luxurious and much-loved Ford Pinto), I found myself boarding the flight to Houston. Fortunately, I had old family friends from Bel-Vue days who were now living there who welcomed me warmly into their home for the first few days of rehearsal. Thank God, as once again I found myself a stranger in a strange land other than for their gracious hospitality. I knew enough to be excited about getting a job at the well-known Alley Theatre, but I knew little more than that. This was the first of many times that I would be "on the road."

I soon discovered a theater with quite an illustrious history and quite the formidable leader in Nina Vance, who, much to my good fortune, was still very much alive and well herself and still serving as the artistic director of the theater which she had founded decades ago. Hers was one of those names that was always on the list when people spoke about the great founders of the regional theater movement along with Zelda Fichandler, Margo Jones, Tyrone Guthrie, Gordon Davidson, William Ball and a few iconic others. I would come to learn that Nina hated the term "regional theater." She would proudly proclaim "Of what are we a region!" And yes, that was more of an aesthetic statement than a question. She believed that these theaters were created by and there to serve their own communities, not to focus on either getting shows to New York or getting shows from New York, but rather creating the art on the stage that she felt was valuable, vital and uplifting for the city of Houston. How the very French songs of Jacques Brel got included in that impressively valid personal mandate for this city in Southwest Texas, I shall never know. But it did mean that even before the date of my graduation from CMU, I actually had a professional job as an actor and was getting a weekly salary to do what I loved. The figure $162.25 is some-how stuck in my mind, equity minimum I am sure, and quite a fortune to me at the time.

A year or two before I arrived, Nina had used her long history of great work in Houston and her considerable Southern charm and savvy to raise the funds to build her theater company a beautiful new home in the newly emerging downtown arts district. And beautiful it was, a kind of contemporary castle with swooping curves, balustrades and bal-conies that housed two sparkling new theaters. *Jacques Brel* was to be the last show of the main stage season in the larger house.

I was probably in rehearsal for the show just a day or two after arriving in the city. Not only was the material completely new to me, but I had the added challenge of going into a company of four made up of three actors who had done the show before in other places, includ-ing Off Broadway. So I was definitely playing catch up in a new city, at a new theater, with brilliant but elusive musical material which often con-fused and confounded me both musically and lyrically! How's all of that for a challenge?

Praise the Lord, everyone was kind and gentle with the new kid on the block. The entire cast, the musical director and Beth Sanford, the director who oddly took that leap of faith when she saw me at TCG auditions in Chicago, all treated me with great respect, kindness and an incredible amount of goodwill and patience. In fact, as I learned many years later, Beth was much more of a champion and defender of mine than I knew at the time. It seems that Nina, who was always lovely and charming whenever she saw me in the hallways, actually wanted to fire me after seeing our first run-through because she did not think that I was up to the enormous skill level of the rest of the company. This cer-tainly helped me to understand retrospectively why I was usually kept behind after the others were dismissed at the end of every rehearsal day to work my solo numbers over and over again. I probably would have fig-ured this out at the time if I had not been so overwhelmed and awed by the entire experience. Ah, the innocence of youth!

Somehow, I got through the rehearsal period without being handed my notice, and the show arrived on its opening night to great acclaim and no apparent dip in the level of the applause during the curtain call when I took my bow. It was so successful in fact that it was extended a couple of times past the original closing date. When the theater's pro-duction schedule demanded that we get out of the space for whatever was next due in the main stage theater, we spent a few days adapting the staging to the smaller theater in the round that was in the basement of the main stage. The demand for tickets was still there, and that second stage was available for the entire summer. In fact, the time came that I actually had to leave the company for my second season of "elite" summer stock back at Pittsburgh Civic Light Opera, where over the course of the summer season I was to play two or three good supporting roles and also be an ensemble member for the others. Just out of school and back-to-back employment already!

Little did I know....

Things would not always be quite that easy or quite that fulsome, and I would later face many a week when I had no work as an actor and did not know when or if I would again. But the Alley and Civic Light Opera gigs were a good start to what was a fairly successful career as a young working actor. Nina Vance somehow learned to love me after that first disastrous run-through, and I returned to the Alley several more times over the next few years. *Jacques Brel...* was kind of the show of the moment in regional—excuse me, Nina—I mean resident theaters and as I now had the show under my belt, or perhaps under my French beret, I did several other productions at other theaters over the next few years. I somehow cobbled together enough work between jobs at several good resident theaters (including a gig at the Papermill Playhouse in New Jersey, playing Puck in *A Midsummer Night's Dream* opposite, believe it or not, Mickey Rooney, a pretty well-known Puck himself, as Bottom) and productions off-off-OFF Broadway to call myself a working actor. The theater gigs were subsidized by a mixture of work on commercials, soap operas and the predictable and much-appreciated weeks of unemployment checks. Lucky me to have enough weeks to qualify for the latter. Between all of the above and a semester and a half of teaching at the American Academy of Dramatic Arts, I somehow managed never to have to take a survival job, as those blissful opportunities waiting tables, bartending and telephone sales were called. I always managed to stay afloat as a working actor who was actually working enough to pay my bills and keep my head fiscally above water. Though not without some heavy treading of water now and then.

However, even with this good fortune, and it was a very good fortune indeed, I was still "hungry." Not literally, thank goodness, but certainly artistically. I was working, and working in good places and making a living. But I was somehow dissatisfied with my lot. Here's an example of why. As a result of kind words and a strong recommendation from some compatriots from my CMU days, I was invited to be a member of the acting company for a production of Shakespeare's *Julius Caesar*, which was being produced by what was at the time the illustrious BAM Theatre Company. It was sort of like Lincoln Center Theatre but a little further south. This was to be quite a high-profile production as the cast included well-known theater stalwarts such as René Auberjonois, Austin Pendleton, Tom Hulce and George Rose, the latter one of the best-known and dearly loved character actors in the New York theater scene. Given the strong reputation of the company during this period, the cast in fact was filled with some of the best and most respected actors in the city. Even with such an attention-getting group, the real focus on this production came from the casting of Richard Dreyfuss, who would play the choice role of Cassius. This was heightened by the fact that Richard had just been nominated for an Academy Award for the movie *The Goodbye Girl*. In a stroke of great timing for the theater, Richard would actually fly back to LA on a day off for the ceremony. When he returned the day after the awards, he headed straight to the theater and passed his Oscar around the dressing room for each of us to hold. So quite a heady time.

However, holding the award statue before the performance that night was truly the high point of what turned out to be a pretty terrible production on every other level. The casting was all wrong (I love Austin Pendleton, but Marc Anthony he is not), the physical production was weird and ill conceived and very little about this incarnation seemed unified or committed in any way. The craziness of it all was epitomized during one performance when George Rose, playing Caesar, raised his arm in an overly theatrical gesture only to be so distracted by the sight of his very modern wristwatch on his arm that he went completely dry and forgot the rest of his monologue. The actor standing next to me whispered loudly enough for most of the cast and perhaps much of the audience to hear, "Methinks Caesar may be late for his assassination today." The level of body shaking that came from actors trying and failing to control explosive laughter probably caused a small earthquake in Brooklyn that day! Clearly this was not one for the ages.

So there I was in an illustrious acting company with one of the most coveted acting jobs to be had in the city at that time, and I could not have been less thrilled or impressed with my situation. Other than by the very handsome paycheck every week. Although that allowed me to pay the bills and not come close to starving, I was "hungry"—artistically hungry and unsatisfied. I was soon to learn that several others in my immediate theater community were having similar feelings.

This propelled me into the next chapter of my theatrical life which would lead to all of the chapters that followed. This chapter was written in a loft space in the Chelsea neighborhood of New York City where, despite extremely humble surroundings and budgets that were lower than low, a group of equally hungry and ambitious friends from my college days were able to make quite a lot of theatrical magic. For a little while on West 18th St, off of 7th Avenue, we were such stuff as dreams are made of....

Off and On Broadway

Watching Julius Caesar being sliced to death while wearing his Rolex watch in Brooklyn really rocked my world. Was this what it meant to be a working actor and part of a highly respected company in NYC? Was this all that it could mean? Or was there, could there be more some way, somehow? While it was glamorous to be holding an Oscar in the dressing room and going out to lunch with the guy who won that Oscar (thanks, Richard, for being so generous about that) and though I was getting a very handsome paycheck for telling Caesar to "Beware the Ides of March"—and yes, as I was given the role of The Soothsayer that actually was one of my lines—something was definitely missing. I was only five or six years out of school and knew enough to know that one had to pay dues to have a career in the arts. I was happy to be securely a working actor at this point, and I was truly not longing for fame or stardom.

But something was missing. I came to realize that it was not fame or fortune that I was after but artistic fulfillment and satisfaction and some greater degree of control over my career. Or any kind of control at all! This was exacerbated by the fact that my time at Carnegie Mellon had pushed me out the door as a classically trained actor at a time when the world was not quite ready to deal with that. Many in the theater field during this era were fairly ignorant of what to do with actors of color outside of the material that was deemed to be "right" for them. I do not exaggerate at all when I tell you that I once auditioned for a production of *Romeo and Juliet* for a very well-known director who asked me to try it once more and make it a little more "streetsy." I believe that I walked out of the room and away from that job. Probably more than once.

I thanked my lucky stars for my good training and my head start coming out of school and going right to work even before graduation. They all provided me with the ability to actually make a pretty good living as a working actor. But even given all of that good fortune, I still had the audacity to want more. Many around me felt that I had so much. I wanted to acknowledge and give full respect to the fact that I was hungry and unsatisfied. An answer to this conundrum began to emerge at a boozy party in the apartment of one of my best college friends Michael Hagerty, attended by Michael's former partner and another schoolmate who I knew to be a talented director, Norman René. As we drank cheap wine and talked deep into the night, I learned that all of us were sharing the same feelings of frustration and hunger for something better. In turn we all told the others that we deserved more and better than what we had received in our careers so far. We knew that perhaps the only sure way to have what we so desired might be to make our own work, to take control of our own destinies.... Whatever that might mean. By early the next morning following our long night of artistic soul-searching, that certainly sounded like a good idea. Maybe it was the cheap wine. Or maybe it was idealism. Maybe it was both!

In the years since graduation all of us had experienced some success and some disappointments in our careers but enough success to know or to talk ourselves into believing that the highs and the lows were not the result of lack of talent and ability. We knew enough about the work that we'd done on the stages at CMU and in the following years to recognize and to trust that we were up to the task of making a play. At some point someone said, "Let's make one!" Years later, Stephen Sondheim would write a song about the exuberance and the not-to-be-defeated spirit of youth called "Our Time." The lyrics of that song described us and this time in our lives perfectly. This was our time! And if the world was not giving us exactly what we needed, then we should make it and give it to ourselves. Bold, brash, incredibly naïve, slightly arrogant, and oh so intense. All of those qualities served us in every good and bad way, but they also pushed us forward. Completely overlooking reality and economics, we pressed ahead, like young colts out of the exercise pen. "We were such stuff as dreams are made of." Off we went, dreaming free!

Perhaps it was our useful enthusiasm or our great ambition. Or perhaps it was merely the economics of actually getting things done in NYC in the late 1970s. Or perhaps it was our mutual burning desire to make our own way in a challenging world. I suspect it was all of the above and a bit more that found us just a few weeks later having miraculously found a play that we thought would serve us well, *The Wager* by Mark Medoff. Somehow we acquired the rights, found a space called

The Nighthouse on West 18th Street in the area of Manhattan called Chelsea, long before Chelsea was Chelsea, and somehow put together enough of our own money so that we could produce this play, cast ourselves in the appropriate roles and begin to be masters of our own domain. Norman led the charge as our director (and quite a good one he was, as proven by a future career that led him to great success at our company, Off Broadway and in collaboration with the gifted playwright Craig Lucas, as well as a few feature films before his death at a much-too-early age). The play had good roles for Michael and me, and the company was filled out by another couple of our Carnegie classmates: John Lantz and Ann Twomey (who later would have great success in a play called *Nuts* in which she was Tony nominated, and in Tennessee Williams's play *Orpheus Descending*, co-starring with Vanessa Redgrave). Quite clearly, CMU had provided us with good training and some very talented friends.

Against all odds, or perhaps just ignoring them all, we got it all done! We rented the space, rehearsed the play, built the set, got ourselves listed in the right places, and opened the play to surprisingly great responses and good houses for our short run. During the last week of performances, our landlord, a stoner named Peter who also owned the answering service (remember those?) that operated in a small office adjacent to the loft and hallway which served as his Nighthouse Theatre, came to us with a proposition. He was no longer interested in using the space for his own purposes—what those were was never very clear—and he was tired of the travails of trying to rent it out on a show-by-show basis. He enjoyed having us in the space and said that he loved our production—though I actually wonder if he ever even saw the play. He was willing to give us an extremely attractive deal to take over the theater on a permanent basis and call it our own. "Sometimes there is God.... So quickly." I suspect that this offer had much less to do with artistic admiration than with supporting a clearly present weed habit and avoiding the problems of being a landlord. Whatever! This was great news for us. Again, naively, blissfully, crazily, bravely and perhaps foolishly we quickly said YES, let's do it. As I said, it was "Our Time."

In retrospect, this all sounds like a bit of a blissful fairy tale, and in many ways it was. But there was a lot of hard work, begging, borrowing and stealing and sweat equity involved. The last element was both figurative and literal, as we spent the long, hot and humid summer after making the deal designing and rebuilding the theater for what would be our permanent use. Those crew skills from our college days came in handy as we somehow managed to turn this pretty grungy loft space into an attractive, sparkling clean and stylish, flexible theater with chairs on movable platforms that allowed us to recreate the space based on the needs of each production and the desires of the directors and designers involved. It was, as I recall, that focus on production aspects and ensuring high quality that helped to define the eventual name of our troupe, which after many a sweaty meeting and a good bit of argument we decided would be The Production Company. Perhaps not the most clever sobriquet, but it was somehow right for us, and as with all names, in short order we became the name and the name became us. It was not long before The Production Company was noted in discussions about the ever-growing Off and Off-Off-Broadway theater scene that was thriving at that time and beginning to highlight some young artists who would go on to great fame and recognition in the years to come. But none of that was in our thinking as we painted, sawed, nailed, cleaned, scrubbed, sweated, argued, laughed, cried and partied over that very long, very hot summer.

Somehow, with the help of several other buddies from Carnegie who joined in on all of the above, we got it all done and in the fall of that year opened this "new" theater with a revival of a play called *Kennedy's Children* by Robert Patrick, which had not been seen in NYC since a brief run on Broadway several years earlier. It was one of those plays that people knew about, but few people had seen. So, between that and somehow scoring a surprising feature story on the ABC local news station and a good review in the *NY Times*, people came! And those 75 seats in our new palace of art were frequently sold out. The phone rang loudly and often, and we happily were on our way. The Production Company was alive and well and living in Chelsea!

I think back on those years at The Production Company as some of the happiest years of my life. And also, quite frankly, as some of the most creative years. The latter I believe stemmed from the fact that we pretty much were creating out of nothing, and for a while at least we expected that nothing would come out of what we were doing except for the joy of making theater. We didn't have any money; there was no real money to be made and no expectation that the "great Art" that we were creating was going to get us anywhere except perhaps to the next production and hopefully another season. I remember the joy and freedom of our creative thinking and our ability to literally make something out of nothing, which we did over and over again. Yes, we certainly sold tickets and hoped for bucks to come into the box office, and we even raised money now and then from friends, admirers and donors. During those years, $100 from somebody was a reason for celebration, and a $500 check actually made us orgasmic. But our real capital resources were creativity, youth, boundless energy, boldness and reckless abandon.

I remember that one of our group had access to a small van. We actually memorized what neighborhoods in the blocks around Chelsea had trash collection on certain days. Armed with that knowledge we would go out the night before and scour the neighborhood for discarded furniture, props that might be useful, almost anything and everything that might one day enhance our productions. In particular I remember that a huge haul of oversized egg crates was brought back to the theater, stored in our now-overflowing basement, and eventually they showed up plastered to the walls of the theater, painted and textured so that under light they became a quite stunning environment that recreated the space in a dazzling way for one of our shows. Our imagination was boundless, and so was our thievery! Is it true that one of these raids led to a police chase with us quickly throwing ourselves into the van and speeding off into the night? Memory is tricky, but yes, I think so. Anything for Art!

We were all happy for a good, long time. Happy and proud of what we had created. The hunger that we all felt went away. It was replaced by exhaustion and new frustrations from time to time, but that was well worth it for our individual and joint feelings of great pride and fulfillment about taking our destiny into our own hands and achieving our little victories. I was happy to have a real artistic home and felt completely fulfilled by playing a number of roles that were hugely satisfying. For the first time of many times to come, I learned that it could be equally satisfying to provide a place for other people to do their work and that I could get as much satisfaction from giving them a place to succeed as I got from being out there onstage myself. It was the latter feeling of satisfaction that led to a huge unexpected shift in direction that would take my now smooth sailing vessel on a completely different course.

As I said, Norman René was designated though initially uncredited as artistic director of our happy company. He directed most of the productions himself. On the occasions when Norman was not filling that chair, we often found ourselves dissatisfied with other directors. I believe that it was at the end of our first full season that Norman, a fellow Scorpio not given to overt praise or boundless acts of generosity, asked me to have coffee with him one afternoon. We had always had a good working relationship and greatly admired each other artistically, but we were never close friends, so this was a bit surprising and somewhat mysterious (another quality that we shared). After a few vague pleasantries, uncharacteristic enough to make us both uncomfortable and slightly impatient with getting to the point, he finally said to me completely forthrightly and incredibly generously, "You know, Sheldon, when I am directing you and we disagree about something, I almost always think that you are right, though I also probably never say that at the time. But you might notice that I usually come back to your point of view or to your idea a day or two later, once I can claim that it is actually mine." I was probably a bit gobsmacked by this revelation (though I suspect that I would never have used that word at the time). After an uncomfortable silence, he bravely continued, "So, I would say that means that you think like a director, that you see the overall picture clearly, and have a great instinct for how to get you, me and the rest of the company to the right place in the rehearsal process." A bit more silence, then, "We keep having trouble finding good directors, so why don't you just start directing for the company. It will be much easier to argue with you about things than it is with a stranger. So, I think you should just do it!"

I am not sure that either of us knew how profound, seismic, or long ranging that conversation was at that very moment. But I did recognize that in addition to problem-solving, Norman was displaying true generosity of spirit and enormous charity in saying all of those things. I don't believe that he meant to actually be urging a career change on me, but in effect, those words almost immediately set me on a new path that would, much to my surprise, be the road that I would travel artistically for the rest of my life.

I started directing at the company just a few months after that (beginning oh so modestly with a very intimate but beautiful production of *A Midsummer Night's Dream* that was truly filled with music, magic and as much mayhem as we could squeeze into our tiny theater space). Much to my surprise, I never stopped and really never looked back nor regretted leaving my burgeoning career as an actor. More quickly than I ever could have imagined I was not only directing all of the time, but I was actually making a living in this new craft. Actually a better and more consistently remunerative living than I had ever had as an actor. Sometimes God and/or a generous friend gives you a shove towards exactly the direction you were meant to be headed all of the time. Sometimes there is both God and the keen eye of a colleague here on Earth so quickly. Lucky for me!

Running a small theater during those years required a great deal of daring, initiative, imagination, talent and now and then a bit of thievery. But as the stakes were economically so low, we were allowed a kind of freedom and abandon to think more freely and creatively. I believe that is what gave the work that came out of The Production Company and many other theaters like ours during that time such vitality. We were all kind of willing to do anything and everything that came to mind.

Given that, and also driven by an economic imperative to bring in funds at the box office, at some point, one of our merry band came up with the bright idea that we should also do "late-night cabaret" performances over the weekends, suggesting that this would be a good way to (hopefully) double our box office income on several days of the week. If we could somehow manage to sell one show at 8 p.m. and another at 11, then the coffers would fill more quickly, which would give us the ability to live on and produce another day. Brilliant idea. Let's do it! There was just one problem. Our space was tiny and included only enough room for the performance area in whatever configuration was being used and the 70–90 seats for the audience on platforms and risers. There was absolutely no wing space. In fact entrances and exits were made from the lobby hallway, or for some shows the acting company had to access the back door entrance which was reached through an alleyway in the basement that delivered you to a small outdoor space behind the building. Woe was us on those performance days when this was necessary during a rainstorm or a blizzard. This meant that there was no place to store or move the set and furniture pieces that were onstage for whatever play was running at the time. So, what to do?

We were not to be daunted! Especially because we now figured out that increasing ticket sales was going to be the rock of our salvation. Even on our lowly budget, economics were still a driving factor in keeping our Art alive. So one, two or all of us came up with the bright idea that rather than trying to cover up whatever was on the stage for the earlier performance we should simply use it as the "environment" for our late-night entertainment. Use the physical space to inspire a context and a raison d'être for the shows that we would do in that late-night series. Once again, necessity was the mother of invention. Rather than just line up four stools and a piano and call it a day, as many cabaret shows were wont to do, we would conceive our shows to really take advantage of having a full set and use that atmosphere as a real character. Or at least to give character to these productions. I'm not at all sure that we knew what we were going to do or how we were going to do it when we came up with this bright fix for our challenge, but we did not let that stop us for one minute.

Forging ahead, the saloon that was the setting for our production of *Kennedy's Children* became a singles bar for our first cabaret show called *Select Any Single*, which used contemporary music to theatricalize the lives of a group of women who meet there every Thursday night to launch their weekend. For another of these late-night shows, the sleek and sophisticated living room set for Noël Coward's comedy *Fallen Angels* stayed almost exactly the same for a show I directed called *Disgustingly Rich*, which almost literally picked up at the end of that play. The show started at the end of a *Fabulous Party* and used songs by the likes of Coward, Cole Porter, Rodgers and Hart and the Gershwins. The servants in the household took advantage of leftover bottles of champagne and booze to throw a fabulous party of their own, often commenting on the behavior of those that they had been forced to serve just a few hours before and then digging deeper into their own lives and emotional realities. It was witty, frivolous, fun and actually did have a life of its own.

This late-night series became enormously popular and got a great deal of attention in the press and the theater community. There were times when it would not be unusual for these shows to be far more popular than whatever play was running, whose set and often props we hijacked for these late-night hijinks! It was actually sometimes very sad to have half a house, or even smaller, at 8 p.m. and then people on a waiting list to get in at 11 p.m. Sad, but kind of wonderful. There were two shows in particular that grew out of this series that gave the theater recognition and also provided strong career boosts for Norman and for me.

Norman and a friend named Craig Lucas, who was still performing then and actually was in the chorus of *Sweeney Todd* on Broadway at the time, somehow convinced the great Stephen Sondheim to open up his trunk of lesser-known songs for their use. With this rich source material, they conceived a two-person show called *Marry Me a Little* that took advantage of the small apartment set for a play we were doing (never to be heard of again) to examine the lives of two forlorn people, alone in their own apartments but sharing the same physical space onstage. With Mr. Sondheim's rich and wonderful material, which was just as popular then as I think it always will be, a clever staging by Norman and lovely performances by Craig and Suzanne Henry, a show came together which immediately sold out for its short run and was moved to a "real" Off-Broadway house just a few blocks away. While it only had a short run there, the show has been produced many, many times over the past decades, and now and then I still hear cuts from the cast album on Sirius Radio. It certainly was one of the shows from the cabaret series that brought our company a lot of attention early on. People started to know and to talk about The Production Company and the work that we were doing with real respect and admiration.

About a year later we were doing the premiere of a new play that I believe was called *Nocturne.* I remember very little about the play except that it was about a jazz musician, a sax player I think, and that it had a raised platform in the back to accommodate a couple of musicians who played an original score during the proceedings onstage. I was somehow designated to come up with the late-night show that would take place during the run of this play, and subsequently it was my task to think of "something" that would be at home in this physical environment. It was not by any means a requirement, but it was also nice to search for even a loose connection between the plays and the late-night shows (as was the case with *Disgustingly Rich*). At some point in my thinking about this, I stumbled on a quote that I believe is attributed to Billie Holiday, who may or may not have actually said "Blues is to jazz what yeast is to bread." I choose to believe that she did utter those words, and whether she did or not, this got me to thinking about creating a show using material from the Blues canon—including Bessie Smith, Alberta Hunter, Ida Cox, and songs that were clearly blues influenced by such masters as Harold Arlen, who to his credit was always the first one to acknowledge that inspiration in his work. Not a bad musical canon to fire off.

It's almost impossible to actually explain the creative thinking that inspires these things, but there was something about the setting for the play, with its three distinct playing areas and its band platform, that led me to thinking about a show that would examine the lives of three different women and a piano player in a cheap hotel and the saloon singer down in the basement using the great songs that I was discovering in my research. Part of that research, by the way, was making frequent trips to a club called The Cookery, where Alberta Hunter was still knockin' them out several nights of the year at the age of 88 or something like that. Amazing! So, of course, a couple of her songs landed in this show, which slowly evolved into something that I titled *Blues in the Night* as an homage to that great song and a summation of the emotional state of the characters.

Not a bad title for this opus of mine. And certainly one that would long be a part of my life for not just years but decades after this show had its opening night of what was intended to be about a ten-performance run on 18th Street at The Production Company. Those songs and the wonderful original cast of the show literally blew the roof off of our tiny theater on opening night. I remember running into the hallway at what I thought was the end of the curtain call only to find myself drawn back into the theater as the audience began to stamp their feet on our fragile platforms demanding an encore, which they were clever enough to quickly improvise and deliver. There are rare but wonderful moments in the theater when you actually recognize that something that you've created might just be life changing. This was one of them for me, and indeed it was. When we started our tiny company we truly believed that "We are such stuff as dreams are made of." And that dream of a night would begin a roller-coaster ride that I am still on nearly 40 years later as I write this. That *Blues in the Night* opening was anything but blue. It was seismic, epiphanic and life changing indeed.

Over the next several decades, in theaters of all sizes all over the country and indeed all over the world, the show was blessed to frequently receive such an enthusiastic response at hundreds of curtain calls. The show would be produced at many of the major theaters all over the country. It would find great success in London, first at the well-respected, small theater called the Donmar Warehouse and then on the West End at The Piccadilly Theatre, and following that at theaters all over the United Kingdom. I personally had the pleasure of directing the show in the UK several times, and I traveled to Japan twice to mount productions. There would later be incarnations with actors of all colors and ethnicities in countries in Asia, South America, Australia and Africa. I write this just a few months after a major revival at The Kiln Theatre in London, which received a Laurence Olivier Award nomination (for the second time), and is scheduled for a move to a West End theater. Certainly none of this was in the wildest of dreams or even contemplated on that great night when the show opened on 18th Street for a limited late-night run.

But first there was the somewhat rocky road to Broadway, and given all of this later success in so many different countries all over the world, a surprisingly less-than-satisfying run on the Great White Way. But even the disappointment of that led to a happy surprise which propelled the show into its long future and gave it such an incredibly long life over the years.

I've written about what a happy, carefree and artistically creative time that was for The Production Company and other Off and Off-Off-Broadway theaters. Especially during those early years when there was a near total and naïve focus on the work itself without any thought to financial remuneration and what would come out of the work outside of actually doing the work and doing it well. I believe that this all started to change and caused a slight death of the artistic purity and creative freedom of those early days when, I believe in the mid- to late 1970s, shows that were created Off and Off-Off Broadway started to move uptown to Broadway houses. This was becoming more and more frequent an occurrence. The most famous example of this is, of course, *A Chorus Line,* which was originally produced in a small house at the Public Theatre and became an international juggernaut after its move uptown to the Shubert flagship theater. Both the immediate and long-term recognition and remuneration that not-for-profit theaters could get from such a move became the focus of a lot of work that was being done and the kind of choices that were made. And why not? All of that could be tremendously valuable to a small theater company. *A Chorus Line* is again a prime example, as the profits from that show filled the coffers of the Public Theatre for years and literally kept the theater alive through good times and bad for many seasons. So, while recognizing the benefits, I also was keenly aware that things were shifting and that the landscape was changing for better and very much for worse.

However, I readily confess that I did not run away from this phenomenon when the Off-Broadway production of *Blues in the Night* got a strong review in the *NY Times* and from several other publications, which attracted the attention of Broadway producers and encouraged them to come downtown to Chelsea to see the show. The one who made the first offer and the one that was the most appealing at the time was from a well-known and successful producer named Burry Frederick, who over the next year or so I would come to refer to as "Blurry"

Frederick—clearly this did not go well. I think that she saw only antici- pated profits in the show and had no real passionate feelings about the material and the musical values of the show at all. This does not make for the best collaboration. I will say that she taught me a good lesson, which is that a lack of genuine passion for a project is always going to lead to lesser results in the long run. Blurry, sorry, I mean Burry, "farmed out" the show over the next couple of years to a number of theaters, hoping to raise the money for the Broadway move. I think her lack of passion was apparent there as well, as she seemed to be able to raise the money for other projects during this same period, while we were kept wait- ing. We first went to the McCarter Theatre in Princeton, a lovely the- ater but far too big and far too grand for the show and nary a person of any color to be found in any audience that we played to over the run. So, not the best home for the show. Following that, we played a short run at a small theater in a small, all-white town in Connecticut—whiter even than Princeton, though I did not think that was possible. Believe me, it is. And finally, at a summer theater in Philadelphia. That space was huge and in the round, so also not ideal from my perspective. But, praise the Lord, we were finally playing to some faces of color, and the show was enthusiastically received by both audiences and critics in Philly. That was the kind of response that our very fancy producer had been saying that the show needed to move forward. When basically nothing hap- pened after that step, it became clear that nothing was going to happen. When I later heard from our stage manager and also a friend of Madam Producer that she had lost interest in the show, I could only respond by saying that this had long ago been prefaced by my losing interest in Blurry (damn, I did it again).

With Norman's encouragement and our combined not-to-be- defeated Scorpio energy, we determined to "rejigger" things by bringing the show back to The Production Company for another run, hoping that either one of the other producers that we'd talked to would return or that others would emerge during this return engagement. Once again, we were met with wonderful audience responses and good reviews from critics. And the producers once again headed to Chelsea.

Eventually, we attracted the interest of Mitchell Maxwell and Alan Schuster, two hugely successful producers and theater owners who were getting attention for their involvement with the Off-Broadway hits *Lit- tle Shop of Horrors, Key Exchange* and an ever-expanding empire of the- aters in the Off-Broadway arena. They took an option on the show and, capitalizing on the success of the second run at The Production Company, very quickly pulled together the financing and got us a Broadway theater. Nirvana!

Well not quite.... The show was very tightly capitalized, too tightly I would say, and had no reserve, so it was do or die on opening night. In addition, the theater was a house called The Rialto. There is good reason to suspect that even die-hard theater fans do not remember this venue. It was actually quite a nice space which had been recently converted from a porn movie house to a legitimate theater, so it smelled (both literally and figuratively) of the unsavory. Its location, on the corner of Broadway and 42nd Street, did not help at all. This was at a time when this location was still part of The Deuce and not the result of the Disneyfication of the area. That was still several years down the road. So, immediately around the corner from the theater were other movie houses that showed the erotic fare that our theater had proffered just months before, and the practitioners of a connected trade were frequently seen on the sidewalks in front of the theater and actually practicing that trade in the alleyway that led to our backstage door. I used to say that it was the only Broadway theater where you could get WHATEVER you want at intermission and with the right, skillful purveyor of the trade, probably make it back in time for the beginning of the second act. So the lack of reserve funds and the nefarious choices of refreshment in the surrounding area of our theater were not helpful.

But prior to that, things went very well. I will say that Mitchell and Alan actually did have genuine passion for the material, real belief in the show, and they were very supportive of me. Working together, we brought together a fine design team and skillful support in the musical department to develop our arrangements and orchestrations. And most important of all, a terrific cast. Wonder of wonders, the company was led by Leslie Uggams (the object of my early life crush from seeing her in "Hallelujah, Baby!"), Ruth Brown, and Debbie Shapiro in the roles of the three women. A pretty dynamite trio, both individually and collectively. The level of superlative singing in the show was apparent from the first day of rehearsal, and it just got better and better every day. Sadly, Ruth Brown who was a true Blues legend was injured during rehearsals and had to leave the company right before we started previews. We flew in Jean DuShon, who was starring in *Bubbling Brown Sugar* in Europe, to step into the show very quickly. (She had done one of the previous incarnations, so she knew much of the material.) Jean was less well known than Ruth but was just as much of a "musical monster" in her own way, so the company stayed strong. All of the elements really came together, and the show looked and sounded fantastic inside of our intimate theater (once you made your way in).

Previews went very well, and our audience responses were strong. Word on the street was good for this show that was sneaking in rather quietly, and the buzz was building. However, we knew that we were dependent on good reviews to push box office numbers up after opening. And we got them! We got many of them in fact. Clive Barnes, formerly the *NY Times* reviewer now writing for the *NY Post*, wrote us an absolute love letter with incredible hit-making quotes. On the whole those were the kinds of notices that we received all around. But not, alas, from Frank Rich of the *NY Times*. His review was, shall we say, not favorable, and we needed that one. Those were the days when a small budgeted show needed a good review in the *NY Times* and/or a big reserve budget, or both, to sustain itself, find an audience and live long enough to catch on and live another day. Lacking either the rave from the *Times* or the fiscal reserves, we closed rather quickly. And after the long, LONG road to Broadway, I confess that this was rather devastating.

I'll also confess now that one of the reasons that we did not get that rave from the *Times* and did not run longer is that the show was just not good enough. Because of the next big "Sometimes there is God" moment in my life, I would have several chances to finally get it right. I had invaluable opportunities to apply my increased knowledge and the suggestions and ideas from others who would come along and help me to carefully craft the show into something that would have an ongoing life over the next several decades. But you only know what you know when you know it. And I just didn't know enough then to form the show into what it would eventually become. Blame for a show not succeeding on Broadway can be and often is placed on any number of things. But, to be totally truthful, the fault was not in our stars but in myself. I was blessed to be able to keep working on the show and to get it right. Eventually, I believe that I did.

This propitious "God" moment would come about nine months after the show closed on Broadway. We'd opened at The Rialto just after the close of the previous season, so any awards eligibility for us would not come around until the following spring. So it came as quite a surprise when I got a phone call months later with the news that *Blues....* had been nominated for a Tony Award as Best Musical of the season.

This surprising news was no doubt the result of some admiration from many on the nominating committee but also the fact that it was a slim season for musicals. *Cats* was nominated in that same year and was, despite many haters, considered to be the front-runner. But I could not have been more surprised ... and more thrilled. Through dogged determination from those same still-devoted producers, there were already plans in the making for a national tour to begin in the fall of that year. The nomination and the stamp of approval from the Broadway community would guarantee that this was going to actually happen. The endorsement also meant that we could extend

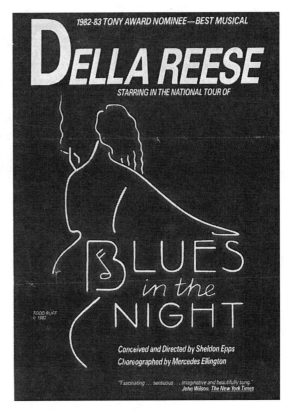

Blues in the Night, **the national tour with Della Reese, circa 1985.**

the bookings for the tour and play more cities. It also brought the much-hoped-for appellation, "The Tony Nominated Musical" to the show, and that would prove useful and valuable in years to come as would another development down the line that also only came about because of this recognition.

As a result of the nomination and the need for smaller-scale musicals in many venues around the country at a time when Broadway musicals were being produced at a larger and larger scale, *Blues in the Night* actually had not one but two national touring companies, each of them with pretty remarkable leading ladies at the helm. Not just remarkable, but legends actually. Della Reese in the first tour and then Eartha Kitt in the second. Not only did I have the joyous experience of working with these two larger-than-life women and luxuriating both in their talent and their remarkable stories—that would have been enough for almost anybody—but this actually gave me an opportunity to keep working on the show. Della, in particular, with her towering knowledge of this canon of music and her sheer sense of what "works" in performance after so many years of being front and center on the stage, offered up many ideas and suggestions which I incorporated into the show, not just for her character but overall, to enormous benefit. In some ways, the tours became a reverse out-of-town tryout for the show (given that it had already had the Broadway incarnation which usually follows the tryout). I learned more, and the show learned more in almost every area. The show that emerged from these tours was admittedly far better than what opened on Broadway. It was the version of the show which was created on the road that had the good fortune to be invited to come to London. Mitchell and Alan, the Broadway producers, showed tremendous loyalty and gratefully stuck with the show throughout the tours. In collaboration with a group of British producers they were able to nail down a slot in the season at the Donmar Warehouse. And it was there that another *Blues...* would sing once more.

Off and On the West End

The Donmar Warehouse was at that time gaining a reputation as an exciting off West End Theatre. A reputation that would continue to grow and thrive when Sam Mendes became artistic director of the theater a few years later and one which has continued over the years. When I arrived in London for rehearsals and went to take a look at the space, the theater immediately felt comfortable and familiar to me. I was immediately at home there because it felt like the older brother or sister of The Production Company. I knew right away that the show would be very much at home in this space and that, if we didn't screw it up, we could have a great success there. Most important and confidence boosting, I knew that the show was so much better because of the benefit of those additional incarnations since the Broadway run. This production would have my greater knowledge of how to make it work, Della's suggestions, Eartha's thoughts and ideas, and the additional benefit of returning to a physical environment which was so very much like the atmosphere in which it had been born. It just felt right. It was a thrill to be doing a show anywhere in London, but the thrill was greater because I was doing this very personal show in this specific theater.

The staff at the Donmar were wonderful and welcoming, especially Nica Burns, who was the theater manager then. (She would go on to run her own West End empire of theaters called Nimax and remained a great friend.) While I felt incredibly positive about doing the show here, I did have a concern about casting the production. I was insistent that one of the roles had to be played by an American Black woman (the part that Della Reese had played so brilliantly in one of the tours). I felt that the part required a kind of sensibility and innate connection with Blues music that I did not think would be found in a British performer. (In later tours and productions of the play I confess that I turned out to be wrong about this.) I convinced the producers to go to the extra expense and effort of bringing Carol Woods, a wonderful singer/actress, across the pond with me. The rest of the company was made up of London-based performers who also turned out to be wonderful. Debby Bishop and Maria Friedman (in one of her first big roles, she got a great deal of attention, and this led to a quite notable career in other West End musicals and on Broadway). The male role was played by Clarke Peters, an American gentleman who grew up in Englewood, New Jersey, the town next door to Teaneck, who was now based in London. Prior to the Donmar production this role had always been played and sung by a gentleman at the piano, who was also the musical director for the cast and band. When we could not find that exact combination in London, Clarke was hired, and his contributions brought wonderful dimensions not just to this character but to the show overall. Being able to fully use the role of The Man in the Saloon and to integrate this great male energy into the show in a more dynamic way both physically and vocally was to my mind the final "revision" in the show that helped to nail the original concept in a way that it had not been fully nailed during the run on Broadway. This very positive change helped to give the show tremendous success in London and beyond.

At every performance that fine cast rocked the Donmar Warehouse. Despite warnings from our producers about British audiences being "a bit more low-key" than crowds we may have played to in America, we were thrilled to have vocal and raucous audiences shouting for more from the very first preview. Carol Woods and I once joked that we never knew that there were this many Black Brits who came to the theater. There weren't. Fortunately for us they just acted like Black folks and responded to the show, the material and the wonderful performances by the cast with hoots, hollers and standing ovations that often shook that theater in the same way that the opening night audience had at The Production Company.

The Donmar production got ecstatic reviews and started to sell out even before we opened. I learned the term "queuing for returns," which meant that there was often a line at the box office waiting for cancellations or no-shows. Our limited engagement sold out very quickly, and shortly after we closed, another show that was scheduled for later that summer fell out, and Nica invited us to return for another Donmar run. We were now returning with strong word of mouth and good reviews already in place, so that run also filled up quite quickly. Again, as at The Production Company years before, buzz started about moving the show to a larger West End venue. Several theaters were interested, and ultimately we decided on the beautiful Piccadilly Theatre, right off of Shaftesbury Avenue. When I expressed some concerns about the theater being too large, it was a lovely surprise to learn that we could restrict sales by not selling seats in the theater's second balcony (or upper circle, as they say over there). Not only that, The Piccadilly also had a "faux" roof which could be raised and lowered and actually made that upper circle seem to disappear. Perfect! Fortunately, we had played many large venues during the tours, so I knew that it could work in this larger configuration. The delightful surprise was that demand for the show was so great that we needed those seats in the upper circle. So we literally raised the roof!

Talk about a warm London welcome. We certainly got that not only at the Donmar but on the West End as well. The show became one to see in London, including with somewhat unexpected audiences. A few weeks into the run I somehow wound up sitting next to Rex Harrison at the performance of another play; I believe it was "Lettice and Lovage" with Maggie Smith. I'd met Mr. Harrison through a college friend who was his assistant when he was doing a play on Broadway. So I boldly leaned over to say hello, expecting it to be a brief exchange. But he was warm and friendly (not always the case, I hear) and asked me why I was in London. When I told him about the show running at The Piccadilly, he said in that entirely distinctive voice which I knew so well from the cast album of *My Fair Lady*, "Blues and jazz? Blues and jazz ... I love blues and jazz!!" and then the real shocker, "Could I come to see the show?" Yes, Mr. Harrison, I think that can be arranged. The next week I was sipping champagne with Sexy Rexy in the VIP room at the theater as he told me that he simply loved act one and couldn't wait to hear more Bessie Smith songs! Ok, how crazy was that? Even in my wildest imagination, it could not get any better than that!

But it actually did get better.

Several months into the run the show was nominated for the prestigious Laurence Olivier Award for Best Musical of the year. And Carol Woods was nominated for best performance by an actress in a musical. Talk about "Wouldn't It Be Lovely?" I can tell you that it was. The long run which started at the Donmar and continued at The Piccadilly also produced a wonderful cast album with the original London cast, a television special of the show, and several subsequent tours of the British Isles and independent productions over the next several years. Just last year the show had a major revival at the new Kiln Theatre and was glowingly received once again, including a second Olivier Award nomination. My London years and the success of the show over there were incredibly sweet to me, with memories old and new of really having the show embraced by the London audiences. That would be delicious enough for any appetite, including my own. But the success of the show in London would produce so much more and push these great songs to be sung for many more years all over the country and all over the world! I'm certainly not the first one to observe that those who run American theaters are frequently Anglophiles when it comes to adoring and worshiping British theater. There is one well-known theater in NYC that at one time in its long life was called the National Theatre USA because of its penchant for bringing over whatever West End produc-

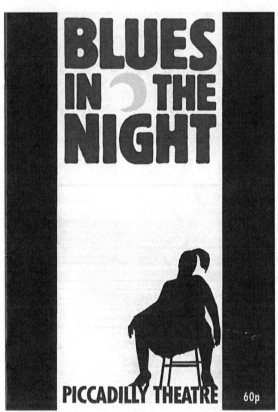

tions and Olivier nominees had been popular the year before. I have found that to be true for many artistic leaders of regional theaters as well. *Blues in the Night* had certainly been gaining attention and renewed reputation as a result of the national tours that took place, but nothing pushed it into the minds of American producers as much as the London productions and the Olivier nominations. Suddenly there were requests from a good number of theaters on this side of the pond to do the show, and the London success certainly spurred the two tours that we did in Japan as well as productions in South America, the British Isles and Australia. I

Blues in the Night at the Piccadilly Theatre in London, circa 1985.

became very appreciative of our national and international taste for all things British in the theater! In fact, over the years there have been so many productions of the show in theaters of all sizes and scale that people now assume that it was a great success on Broadway. I believe that the Tony nomination, the London success and the cast album, which became pretty popular, are responsible for this impression. And so be it! I've come to be rather proud of the fact that a show that had a rough road to and short run on Broadway has had such a long life all over the world. Despite what one hears, it can happen!

Over the next several years I directed numerous productions of the show at many of the major resident theaters all over the country. It became something of a calling card and a door opener and truly established my freelance career and kept me going quite nicely between directing fees and the royalties that came in as the conceiver of the show. This was great but also overly seductive. After about four or five years of being "on the road" with *Blues....* I recognized that I could easily become a kind of one-trick pony, a phenomenon that I had observed with some of my compatriots and one which I had come to fear. I'd watched some of my colleagues become far wealthier than I was from doing a specific, well-known show over and over again but rarely being asked to do anything else. This could be a lucrative but dangerous road, and it was certainly one that I was not eager to travel. Somewhere along the line when yet another theater called asking me to come and mount a production of the show for them, I screwed my courage to the sticking point and said no. Not easy, but a wise choice that led me to pushing myself or being pushed by others into broadening the scope of my directing ventures in a healthy and productive way. Getting off the *Blues in the Night* road, much as I loved it, took me in new directions both literally and artistically. And those paths ultimately led to my "Artistic Homes." Both the first one and the one which I would occupy for 20 years.

Movin' On, Movin' Up

It has been my experience that "Leaps of Faith" are frequently necessary for a life in the theater. I'd broaden that to say that they are necessary for a productive and profitable life, period! My father had taken a great leap of faith when he moved to what was then the "Wilds of California" to establish Bel-Vue Church so many years ago—against both the good wishes of my mother and without her permission or approval. In fact, there was a period of time when she declared that she had no intention of moving with him to that Wild West frontier. But thank God they got over that; otherwise, there would have been no Little Me! His leap of faith worked out pretty well for all of us. So willingness to risk falling in order to fly was just in my blood I guess, and for the most part it has served me well.

When I decided to put the brakes on directing *Blues in the Night*, I realized that I was also risking the bread and butter directing fees that had come my way from so many theaters. That risk was frightening but necessary. I also knew (and still know) that it is the tendency of the American Theater field to assign artists, especially young artists, and even more especially artists of color, to aesthetic boxes that describe exactly who they are and what they do. These assignments may or may not correspond to what they actually do and assuredly may not apply to what they want to do. But it can become a box that is difficult to escape if one is not careful and deliberate.

Boxing you in like that is just a convenient and often minimizing way for those in hiring positions to view you and your work. As one who had very broad artistic desires and wide-ranging tastes, a legacy of my very theatrically diverse training at Carnegie Mellon, I knew enough to be shaken up when I heard that someone recommended me to direct a play, and the reply of the producer was, "Sheldon Epps, he just does those Black musicals, right?" I knew that this perception of who I am and what I do could well be a kiss of death at worst and incredibly limiting at best. I had nothing against Black musicals and indeed had grown up loving them. But I had no desire to have that short summation become the thing that defined my artistic choices and opportunities. It was time to take that particular leap of faith and fast!

As I have often said, I never wanted to be categorized as a Black director. In the way that term is used and interpreted in our field it is, by intention or not, demeaning and intended to be diminishing of one's abilities and is probably "ghetto-izing." The fact is that I have never heard my colleagues of the lighter hue described as White directors. They were simply directors or choreographers.

There was a not untrue generalization that was often whispered in very Black humor terms which broadcast the fact that almost any Black director could get a job working in some regional theater somewhere during the month of February, because it was during Black History Month that most theaters programmed their "Black slot" for the season. A nice guarantee, I suppose, but beyond being limiting in terms of the range of material that one was offered, I felt perhaps an arrogant desire to work during the other months of the year as well. Call me crazy, but that was the kind of career building I was interested in. So, think of me not as a Black director but as a director who has the good fortune to be a Black man in America who has wide range but also the benefit of bringing that sensibility, history, culture, musicality and finesse to the work, no matter the ethnic or cultural specifics of the project. Believe it or not—and it is true whether you believe it or not—at that time a little over a decade before the turn of the century, this was still quite a revolutionary idea. So I set out on a road with the aim of fighting that artistically tight perception. This covert kind of thinking was less charitably described as the dark secret of the American theater—this ghettoizing of artists of color in our supposedly highly evolved, liberal and open-minded field. If it was truly that, the fight that I had on my hands would not have been necessary. But the minds were not merely as open as they pretended to be and not nearly as liberal or evolved as they frequently protested. So I had to wage that war and make "Good Trouble" in that fight for many, many years early in my freelance career.

And so it was that I had to broadcast that intention rather loudly and I suppose somewhat hubristically in order for that message to be clearly heard in the years before I landed in my first artistic home. It was not at all then or now that I had any problem or lack of desire to do the plays of Black playwrights and/or to work with artists of color. In fact,

I loved that. That was comfortable, welcoming, warm and rewarding. It is only that this was not the only thing that I wanted to do and certainly not the only thing that I wanted the theater world to tell me that I was capable of doing! I wanted and needed the same artistic freedom to roam the world of the theater that my white colleagues enjoyed automatically. I had to fight for that right, and I did! I ultimately directed a play (written by a Black writer by the way) that spoke of the Southern Arrogance of certain African Americans. Though I had never lived in the South, my roots were there, and I confess that I inherited that quality both from my parents and my ancestors. That arrogance served me well, and it also frightened some people. But it could be quite useful and frequently was called upon to make my point in making this fight.

Knocking on doors with that in mind did get results, and I quickly got a reputation for being up to the task with new plays and old as well as musicals, whatever the "roots" of the material. However, it remained tricky. An example......I quite successfully directed that quintessentially WASP play *The Philadelphia Story* by Phillip Barry at one of our major theaters (NOT the all-Black version which some colleagues stupidly thought I would be mounting.... What?!). The production was beautifully done by all involved and set box office records for the theater. The next year the very same artistic director who had graciously invited me to direct that play called and asked me to do a play in the February slot. Oh yes, that again. While I admired the work of the Black playwright that was presented to me, I asked out of curiosity more than anything else, "What else are you doing in the season?" When I was told of the other choices, I believe that I told her that I would really rather do *Twelfth Night*. This statement was followed by a long, pregnant pause. Finally I asked her if she thought that I was not up to that one, and please tell me honestly if that is the issue. "Oh no, not at all. That's a perfect play for you. But if you directed the Shakespeare play that would mean that I would have to have two Black directors in the season." Another long pause.... And then I said with all the icy chill that I could muster, "In all the years that you've been an artistic director, has it ever occurred to you to position having two White directors in one season as a problem?" The longest pause of all. A really long one! Followed by, "You know, you're right. I'm quite embarrassed that I said that to you. I really need to think about that." I never heard from that artistic director again. Southern Arrogance was on display and may have cost me that job. But the point was made. Whether she ever operated differently in the future, I cannot say. But I do believe that the point was made.

Experiences such as that one made the satisfying and rewarding career that I was having quite frustrating and angering. I had flashbacks of the director who had asked about my making the Shakespeare character "more streetsy." That kind of ignorance and covert racism was shocking, far too prevalent, appalling and sadly enervating. All of this for a person who was doing very well in his career. What was it like for my brothers and sisters of color who were not blessed with the great opportunities I was having?

Even more, this kind of racism, the "Dark Secret of the American Theatre," exacerbated another challenge that I was facing: constant life on the road. Another production, another city, another hundred people to meet and greet, and another few weeks living out of a suitcase. Such is the life of a freelance director. And the more success you have, the more you are on the road. I certainly could not complain about the great opportunities that came my way at the illustrious Guthrie Theater, Cleveland Playhouse, Seattle Repertory Theatre, Arena Stage, Coconut Grove Playhouse in Miami, Walnut Street Theatre in Philadelphia, and many, many others. These were theaters that I'd admired and heard about for years. For example, I had the dreamlike experience of being in the rehearsal room and directing on the distinctive stage founded by Tyrone Guthrie at the theater that now was named in his honor. That was my great honor to be sure. The work was wonderful, wide ranging and creatively rich and rewarding in all of the ways that one hoped for.

But the lifestyle was tiring. The successful freelance life meant almost never being at home in your real home. It was a constant cycle of packing a bag, going off to a new city to work at a new theater. Living in an apartment with the same corporate furniture and white walls with bad artwork—or no artwork, just bare white walls. Rehearsing and opening a production at the theater, then getting on the plane, usually the very next day to return to home base for a few days or a gracious couple of weeks and then starting the same cycle all over again and returning to another theater-supplied apartment with the same bad artwork, corporate furniture and the very same white walls.

After a few years of this theatrical merry-go-round, I literally remember waking up some mornings with the need to figure out and remind myself of what city I was in this week. This artistically fulfilling career that I was having was exciting and rewarding in many, many ways. But it was also mentally and emotionally exhausting and certainly hell on establishing any kind of long-term relationships, which I fervently believe are necessary to feed the heart, soul and body of one's work. At the start of this cycle I recall running into a well-known elder director who had been leading this kind of professional life for many years. He was respected and valued in the field. But as we sat and talked and he told me about his recent gigs and the jobs that were coming up which involved leaping back and forth across the country, he seemed to turn gray or even more gray in front of me, and his eyes went more dead as he rolled out this litany of cities that was before him over the next season. I left that conversation depressed, tired and exhausted. I suspect that I needed a stiff drink and a nap later that day. My own personal cure for depression has always been a good, long nap. I needed one badly after that conversation!

The idea that this would be the life ahead of me for the next decades was exhausting. As the ladies of the dance hall sing in a well-known musical comedy, "There's gotta be something better than this!" But what? I spent many sleepless nights and restless naps examining possible options.

During this time of artistic restlessness, I had my initial directing opportunity at Pasadena Playhouse. Just as we were about to go into previews for that play I got a call from someone on the staff of the Old Globe theatre in San Diego. They were asking about my availability and interest in directing a new play called *Mr. Rickey Calls a Meeting* that would begin rehearsing just a few weeks after the current show opened. The Old Globe was certainly one of those theaters that was high on my list, and I had heard great things about their illustrious Artistic Director, Mr. Jack O'Brien. But I was just plain tired and could not bear the thought of one more set of white walls and struggling to remember where I was. Even though this invitation was very attractive, I politely declined.

The next day, that artistic director himself was on the line, immediately turning on what I would come to know as the "reliable O'Brien charm," wit and good humor. He told me that he certainly understood how I felt and recognized that kind of weariness having experienced it himself earlier in his career when he, in his words, was so jonesing to direct that he would go anywhere and everywhere to do it. Receiving emotional understanding and empathy rather than argument and pressure is in and of itself incredibly charming and persuasive. Well done,

Jack! He suggested that perhaps I could come down to San Diego on my day off just to see the theater, perhaps have lunch and talk more about the play. I still wasn't sure that I wanted to pack those bags again so quickly, but I thought that a nice train ride along the Pacific would be a fun and relaxing way to spend the day off. So, once again, why not? I could always still say thanks but no thanks.

At this point it will come as no surprise that I did not say no to that day-long trip to the beautiful city of San Diego where I discovered very quickly the physical, aesthetic and creative joys of the magical kingdom of the Old Globe. The theater is located in the center of one of America's most beautiful parks in a city which can boast of some of the most crystalline sunny days that you will find in our country. All of this simply took my breath away. The apartment where I would stay might still have white walls, but everything else about this place was glorious. The theater spaces (all three of them), the gorgeous park surrounding the theater, the shops, the gracious plazas in front of the theaters, and perhaps most glorious of all, Mr. O'Brien himself! We'd never met, though I certainly was well aware of the name, and I had seen his award-winning production of *Porgy and Bess* years before. I immediately discovered in Jack as kindred a spirit as I could hope to find. He was energetic, smart as a whip, passionate about our work, persuasive without letting you know that you were being persuaded, and wickedly funny. This Jack very much deserved his name as he was both nimble and quick! Whatever happened with the play, which I also thought was pretty persuasive, the idea of getting to spend more time enjoying the pleasure of his company in this magical and dazzling theatrical kingdom was as attractive as Cleopatra was to Antony (a play that they were not producing at that moment, but they could have been in that gorgeous outdoor Elizabethan theater). I was hooked and probably got over myself and any internal debates I was having between me and me, and I signed the contract before I got back on the train! I look back on that change of heart as one of the best decisions I ever made.

So, I went back to Pasadena, opened the play, returned home for about a week, repacked my trusty bag, got on another plane and returned to San Diego to start rehearsals at the Old Globe. Not surprisingly the apartment walls were indeed empty, bland and white. But nothing else about the theater and the life that I would have there ever could be described in those terms.

While packing my bags to head out to California to start rehearsals at the Old Globe, I would never have guessed that much of my life over the next five years would be spent at this theater. The most I hoped for was a good rehearsal period and a production that met with enough success that it might lead to an invitation to direct at the theater again in the future (always a hope for a freelance director). All of that would happen, but there was much more in store for me in what would be a vitally important collaboration and learning ground that would provide me with a number of major turning points in my career. And some bumps in the road as well. But I had come to expect that from even the most rewarding life in the theater.

Mr. Rickey Calls a Meeting was a fascinating and powerful play by Ed Schmidt. The idea for the play was taken from one line in an autobiography, no doubt ghostwritten, of Joe Louis. He said that as Branch Rickey, the renowned baseball manager, was contemplating bringing Jackie Robinson up to the major leagues, he hoped to gain the approval of the most well-known Black men of that era. So an invitation went out to Joe, Bill Bojangles Robinson and Paul Robeson to discuss the issue and celebrate his wise decision. Mr. Rickey assumed there would be enthusiastic consensus from this illustrious crowd but had underestimated the complicated and combative reactions that he would get from Mr. Robeson. Drama ensues.

There is a strange and wonderful dynamic that can sometimes occur with plays when something from the outside world is infused into the process. That happened with this production. We were in our second or third preview when the Rodney King verdict came down. The massive injustice of that decision ignited the emotional realities of the gifted and volatile Black actors in the company and charged the play and those gigantic characters with a blazing combination of fury, indignation, frustration and righteous anger which lifted a play already full of racial fireworks to a nearly explosive place. The performances on that preview night, at the opening and throughout the run carried those emotions into the text and the explosive situation of the play. That horrible but relevant event completely changed the experience for all of us and for our audiences. The play now had a powerful subtext which made it immediate and perhaps more powerful than it would have been had we not opened at a time when riots were breaking out all over the country as a response to the racial injustice of the moment. Such is the power of live theater.

The run of the play at the Globe was a great success and would lead to many other productions for the play in ensuing years, including a radio play version that has remained popular and is often used as a teaching tool in various academic programs. That led to a swift invitation to return to the theater the following year, this time to direct Shakespeare's lesser-known play *All's Well That Ends Well* in the beautiful Elizabethan outdoor theater that I had admired so much on my first quick visit.

This initial success at the theater had served me as I had hoped. What served me equally well and more vitally for the long run was furthering my collaborative relationship with Jack. He was generous with his time, and we quickly connected over many shared interests and a mutual affection for the dishy dinner served up with a couple of cocktails. But what really drew me to him artistically and aesthetically was his wide-ranging theatrical tastes. When I arrived for rehearsals for my first play there, Jack had just finished directing *King Lear,* with a monumental performance by Hal Holbrook, and was about to start rehearsals for *Damn Yankees* (a production that would ultimately move to Broadway). I certainly wanted to be around an artist who had that kind of range which, of course, was then reflected in the programming of the theater. A typical Old Globe season would include musicals, new plays, Shakespeare, Ibsen and August Wilson. This was a place for me, and it might (and indeed it did) offer me the opportunity to cover that same broad range in my own work. So I was happy to quickly be considered a member of the family. Flashback to young Frankie in that early-going theater experience; this could certainly be a place where I could find "The we of me" and be very much at home theatrically.

In one of those moments of divine synchronicity, an opportunity came along that would allow that desirable situation to become a reality, and a chief player in making that happen was a blast from my past, Theatre Communications Group. It was TCG that helped me to make the leap from student to working professional after graduation from Carnegie so many years before. And at this moment, it was the generous support of TCG and the Pew Charitable Trust through a program called the National Theatre Artists Residency Grant that would allow me to call the Old Globe my artistic home for the next several years. These highly competitive grants provided enough guaranteed financial support for artists to feel comfortable committing to being at one theater for a minimum of four to six months a year. It took the pressure off of chasing after enough productions in any season to fill up your schedule and your bank account. That very attractive situation meant a lot less packing and repacking and far fewer of those bare, white walls in a constantly revolving list of cities. This was, in fact, exactly what I was looking and hoping for. An end to that dreaded feeling of waking up unsure of what city you were in because of the endless moving from place to place that came with life on the road. Getting this grant was not a life changer, but it did mean that life could be different for at least a couple of years. Beyond the money, the grant also meant that I would have a place where I was valued and trusted as an artist and where I would have some measure of control over what I would direct. Always based on the theater's needs to be sure but also with at least some possibility of fulfilling my own aesthetic desires and my needs for my personal artistic growth. All of this made scoring one of these grants incredibly valuable. So there was a great deal of celebration and glee when we received the grant for an initial two-year period and even more when an extension of the funding was announced and we were granted a two-year extension of this precious collaboration.

In short order and after several conversations, Jack and I decided to use the grant to create the position of associate artistic director. While the theater had previously engaged several artistic associates, there had never been anyone in this high-ranking position. And frankly, it was needed and necessary. As I said, the theater had three beautiful performing spaces and a year-round season. This means that over the course of a year, the company produced anywhere from 12 to 15 productions as well as readings, workshops, children's programming and supported an MFA Acting program. That's quite a lot for one man to oversee (although Jack did have over most of his years there the valuable advice and assistance of Craig Noel, his predecessor who was still active and sharp as a tack).

Given this exciting but heavy load, Jack was eager and ready to have someone on staff that he trusted to help keep all of the balls in the air. There was another reason that my tenure at the theater in this newly established position was ideal at that very moment in time. Shortly after I arrived to begin my residency at the theater, Jack was Broadway bound to direct the transfer of *Damn Yankees*. This meant that between rehearsals and previews for that production, he would be mostly in NYC for a period of a little over three months. Basically I was the proverbial baby thrown into the middle of the pool, learning to swim quickly right after I settled in. It was only a few weeks later that Jack said, playfully but also quite seriously, "Well, you got it, honey. Try not to fuck it up!" Ever encouraging, ever supportive, and also ever so wicked! I do not mean to imply that he was leaving me to run the theater and move into his office. That was not the case (although, like a directorial Eve Harrington I may have sneaked in there from time to time and sat in his chair in front of his mirror!). There was a very capable management and production staff in place that was fully capable of keeping the ship smoothly sailing forward. But it did mean that I was frequently asked to "go on" in his place for fundraising events, board meetings, rehearsals, production meetings and the famous "Company Calls" which took place when two or three new shows were going into rehearsal to welcome the new artists to the theater. I did not get to BE the artistic director, nor was I in any way ready to be, but I did get the opportunity to function as an artistic director. The cavalier and generous way in which Jack not only allowed this to happen but actually pushed for it was a measure of his belief in me and also of his own very clear level of security both as an artist and as the leader of the company. As a result, it was here at the Old Globe that I got my MFA in "The Art of Artistic Direction." A degree that, though I did not know it at the time, I would come to appreciate and put to use for many years very quickly.

And then there was getting to direct all of the time. Or at least two or three times over the course of a season. Sometimes there were "assignments," those projects that were in place before my arrival that I suddenly inherited. But in most cases, they were projects of my own choosing. I would offer up titles and/or playwrights that I wanted to explore, and if all things worked out in the formation of the season, then I had a full pass to choose exactly what I wanted to do. My first production in my new position was, by assignment, a new production of *Blues in the Night*. I actually fought that a bit, but Jack felt that it was important for me to be introduced in my new position with what he called "your signature." I accepted and understood that, and we opened the season with a handsome, beautifully performed and hugely successful production of the show. Over the next years, I followed this with a range of work that ran the gamut of theatrical literature including Noël Coward, Tom Stoppard, Shakespeare, and Ibsen. The latter was an "ahead of its time" production that featured nontraditional casting of his masterpiece *Hedda Gabler*. The incredibly gifted CCH Pounder played the title role brilliantly. I have seen many other Heddas before and since. Others have been as good, but nobody has been better. And certainly, hers was a sui generis performance that has not and cannot be matched. A few seasons later the world premiere of a new musical came along in my final year at the Globe that proved to be significant. Its success in ways both simple and complicated had me traveling in another direction and moving away from this comfortable home.

I learned so much during my time at the theater from covering this huge landscape of material. My residency there and the artistic freedom and allowance that I was given to spread my wings soon eradicated the outside world's designation of me as a "Black Director." Yes, it had taken that long to erase something which, to my mind, should never have existed. But finally I was simply recognized and indeed celebrated as a talented director in the field who was making a difference. Not just with the quality of work that I was doing but with the range of that work. That was a battering ram tearing down those strong walls. I was happy about this for me, to be sure. But in larger terms, this opportunity did begin to enlighten others and change perceptions. This door opening (or door crashing) was beginning to result in far more opportunities for directors and artists of color to be designated for slots in regional theaters in months other than February, doing work from a much larger canvas based on their needs and desires for their growth and expansion. To be clear, I never felt that an artist should have any hesitation about doing work only by those of the same color if that was what they wanted to do. Indeed, I would have some of the best experiences of my life directing plays or musicals by Black playwrights. It was my belief then and now, however, that the gift of ethnicity should be exactly that, a gift and not a restriction. White directors, be they English, Irish, French or Mid–Western, Eastern or Southern American, were free to explore the entire canon of world literature (ironically Black plays included). That is also as it should be. I just wanted, and in fact demanded, that same artistic latitude for myself and for all directors of any color. I believe that I helped to make some strides in that direction and to pull down some walls. Believe me, those barriers are still up in a lot of places. Far too many. Shockingly they exist either literally or emotionally in the hearts and minds of far-too-many leaders of our American theaters. But it is better. As I heard my elders say many times when I was young, "We ain't where we want to be, but thank God, we ain't where we was!"

So, there was much to be proud of. Theatrically, politically and even racially. There were so many people involved with this theater including board members, staff, subscribers and others who literally had their first contact with a Black man in a position of authority during my time there. And so many who were introduced to an even wider range of work by artists of color than they had been given the opportunity to appreciate. I guarantee you that very few if any of them had ever seen or even vaguely contemplated the notion of a Black woman playing Hedda Gabler, for example. Barriers, perceptions and racist attitudes were attacked by me and many others and that caused those walls to come tumbling down. I am very happy to have been one of the wall batterers! That was a noble task that would continue.

The brilliant CCH Pounder as Hedda Gabler at the Old Globe theatre, 1995 (photograph by Ken Howard).

And, oh yes, there was also that new musical. In so many ways Mr. Shakespeare was very much at the heart of much of the work at the Old Globe. And in fact his canon of work had touched my life for many years. During my training at Carnegie, in my early career as an actor and director, and now here in this first artistic home. When Jack urged me early on to "Think of something BIG that you want to do, honey. Something really big and bold," that's the kind of encouragement and urging that you want from an artistic director but rarely get. Usually the first questions being asked, and not in a hopeful way, are how large is it, how many characters, how big a band? Jack pushing me in the BIG direction got me thinking about my favorite Shakespeare play. Which one? Here is a hint: "If music be the food of love, play on!"

ACT V, SCENE TWO

Back to Broadway

By the time I was in residence at the Old Globe, my parents had retired and moved back to my mother's birthplace: Windsor, North Carolina. Though fiercely independent my mother, Kathryn, like many wives and mothers of her generation, had followed my father's path as he built his career. She certainly had a rich life of her own, including a highly successful career as a school teacher. But when he needed to make a move for career reasons, she generously followed. And so it was that she begrudgingly moved to California when he had the calling to establish his church in Los Angeles, not at all willingly; they actually separated for a while. Fortunately for my family she did eventually follow, and they established an ongoing life together that lasted for 66 years of marriage. Less reluctantly, but still with some qualms, she and the entire family moved to the east coast when my father had another calling to the administration of the Presbyterian Church which was located in New York City. As she had generously been a follower, willingly or not, when my father was approaching retirement age, he graciously and quite wisely asked her where she wanted to live. Where did she want to spend the last years of their long life together? My mother, though she enjoyed the pleasures of New York City and the fancy life, said that she just wanted to go back home. Back to the South, to be close to her family and friends in her hometown. My wise father quickly accepted that proposition, and they built a comfortable home on the outskirts of Windsor where they lived quite peacefully and happily until they both passed away at the amazing age of 98!

Why do I bring this up now? What does all of this have to do with the title of this chapter? It's because my road back to Broadway and destinations beyond actually started in the woods behind their lovely home in this small, Southern town which provided not only great food but also frequent inspiration. These woods, which truly were "lovely, dark and deep," were also a place of peaceful contemplation for me on my trips back to North Carolina to visit them. Both for inspiration and the good food!

Just before one of those visits I had another encouraging conversation with Jack about what's next for me at the Globe. I had seen a production of *Timon of Athens* in New York that made use of a score by the great Duke Ellington that was drawn from his *Shakespeare Suite.* I'd long wanted to return to one of my favorite plays by The Bard and had in mind making use of material from Ellington's huge canon of music in that play. On a walk in the woods one day inspiration and clarity came suddenly together in a way that can frighten and inspire you at the same time. I very clearly had a vision of *Twelfth Night,* Ellington songs and Har-

Play On! at the Brooks Atkinson Theatre on Broadway, 1996.

lem in the 1940s that was both blazingly clear and wonderfully elusive all at once. Somehow I knew right away that there was a musical to be born from that combination, and I knew that that musical would be called *Play On!* Have I said this before, "Sometimes there is God..."? I honestly do believe that blasts of inspiration like that are truly Heaven-sent.

Shortly after that fateful stroll in the woods, I returned to home base at the Globe and got to work. Rereading the play, which I knew well from playing Feste twice when I was an actor and seeing many, many productions over the years, but I read it again ... many times. I researched the Harlem Renaissance in tons of books and luxuriated in the glorious art that came out of that period. Romare Bearden, Archibald Motley, Miguel Covarrubias and many more provided images that screamed with brilliant and inspiring theatricality. Most of all, I spent hours digging into the music of the great Mr. Ellington using every pre-internet source that was at my disposal. Even I who prided myself on knowing this era of music well was surprised to discover the true breadth, scope and variety of his work. He truly had touched every musical base from classical to Blues to sacred music, and he even wrote scores for films and lesser-known Broadway musicals. I was simply blown away and overwhelmed by how much was available.

That was a good thing indeed as I'd made a vow to myself that I would very strictly follow the sacred rule of musical making that the songs had to advance the story. I was not interested in doing a well-put-together Ellington revue. I wrote a scenario based very clearly on Shakespeare's text and characters (even down to their names), and I wanted to be sure that at those moments when the characters burst into song that they burst into songs with lyrics and musical feel that actually made sense for the dramatic moment. I made a vow to myself that if I could not do that and do that honestly, I would not proceed with the project.

Two things made any thought of giving up on it totally unnecessary. First, there was the breadth and volume of the master's songs that existed in numerous recordings by such a wide range of artists. That quickly yielded up a treasure trove of material that gave me many of the songs that I needed for many of the musical placements. But there were spots where I could not find what I felt was exactly the right song. Or at least I had not found it yet.

Help came from a good friend named Mercedes who had worked with me as choreographer on several productions of *Blues in the Night*. I wanted to work with her again on this project because she is a fine collaborator and rather expert in the moves and music of this period, including the tap vocabulary of the era. No less vital, her last name is Ellington. She is the granddaughter of Duke and the daughter of Mercer who was leading the famous and still-popular band by this time. Clearly this woman literally had this great music in her blood and in her soul. I told her about my concept, which she immediately, enthusiastically embraced, and also about my strict guidelines for the use of the songs. She asked me if it would be helpful to have a printout listing of all of Ellington's songs. Anticipating a good number of pages, I told her that this would indeed be helpful. A few days later Mercedes delivered to me a stack of paper that was in fact HUNDREDS of pages long! Clearly his range was inexhaustible. Yes indeed, having that was certainly useful. I soon discovered that Mr. Ellington would never fail me as a collaborator. If I kept looking long enough, I would discover something in his incredible canon of music that "fed" the moment not only lyrically but also with the tone, feel and musical texture that was needed. Because the man wrote everything! As I continued my work on the show, I would sometimes play a game and challenge the Duke with producing the right song for a particular moment. It was always about my digging further and never about his not being up to the challenge. If I kept searching, prodded transcendentally by my collaborator, he would certainly provide what was needed. Over and over again.

This did not mean that I was always looking for the unknown, though it was always a pleasure to find what I call a hidden gem. Some of the better-known songs were perfect for the course of the action such as "Mood Indigo," "I Got It Bad and That Ain't Good," "In My Solitude" or "Drop Me Off in Harlem." But there was also gold to be discovered and mined in lesser-known masterpieces such as "Something to Live For" and especially "Rocks in My Bed," a rollicking blues song that would eventually stop the show at every performance of every production because it was so perfectly right for that specific moment and for those specific characters (imagine Feste the Jester and Sir Toby Belch as two older Black gentleman given to the joys of women, drink and self-pity lamenting their current state in a blues-tinged duet).

Armed with the possibility of this wonderfully theatrical and inventive score I continued to flesh out the story and characters. I reached a point where I felt that I had a clear road map in terms of structuring the story. I'd always known that I wanted to find a strong collaborator to work on the actual book with me, and I specifically wanted someone with a great ear for dialogue. I turned to the talented writer Cheryl West, whose play *Jar the Floor* had been presented at the theater a year before. I knew that I needed a writer whose language had its own kind of music, tone and literal and figurative color to give these Shakespeare-inspired characters true musical theater life. Based on what I'd seen in her play and some of Cheryl's other work, I felt that she was exactly the right person to become a part of this team that included Shakespeare, Duke Ellington and me. She was honored to be asked and very much up to the task. Cheryl took my treatment/scenario and a compilation CD of the songs that I'd made and went to work. She "got it" immediately. Even better, as I had hoped, she was a generous, kind, inventive and joyful collaborator.

We worked well together and we worked swiftly but carefully. We joyfully arrived at a place in our work where we felt ready to present our ideas and a draft of the script to Jack and others on the production staff at the Globe. It was immediately embraced by all, and we decided to put it on the calendar for the upcoming season. This was all going very smoothly. Maybe too smoothly.

One of the truths that I learned during my time at the Globe, a truth which would serve me well in years to come, is that artistic ambitions and dreams often meet a formidable foe in the shape of economics. We were dealt a body blow by that evil monster when the seasonal budget was examined, and we all had to recognize and admit that the additional costs of doing the first production of a new musical at the theater were blowing us out of the water. Extra money was going to be needed to make it a reality on the stage of the main stage theater and to support the show as it would need to be nurtured and birthed. This was not the end of the road, but it was going to be a road delayed. Much like the dream deferred of the poem by Langston Hughes. But I was determined not to let this dream dry up like the well-known "raisin in the sun," and the only place that it was going to "explode" would be on the stage at the Globe. Even if that meant a little patience and another season going by, so be it!

Ken Denison, the production manager at the theater and a good friend both then and now, helped me to manipulate things so that we could have a reading of an early draft of the show in NYC. The intention was to further develop the material, which was healthy, but also a way to go fishing for some enhancement funding from a commercial entity to support the initial production. Ken and I made that happen through combined determination and probably a bit of slyness about what we were up to. But we made it happen. A very bare bones reading took place putting forward the concept and, of course, those great songs. As with many such events, audience reaction can be boisterous and supportive but still leave the cash drawer empty. In this case we got both the audience reaction we wanted and the financial support that we needed

Cheryl Freeman and the ensemble in the first production of *Play On!* at the Old Globe theatre, 1996 (photograph by Ken Howard).

thanks to the immediate offer of support from my former collaborators on *Blues in the Night*, Mitchell Maxwell and Alan Schuster. Not so coincidentally, this reading took place while they were enjoying a great success with the revival of *Damn Yankees* that Jack O'Brien directed. That production was now happily running on Broadway. Sometimes it really is all in the family. With their commitment to provide enhancement funding in exchange for the right of first refusal to move the show after its initial production, we were ready to go ahead once again, and the show was back on the schedule for the following season. This raisin was not drying up and now needed to be prepped to explode.

During the early days of the casting process for any show, the casting director will often ask you to offer up your "wish list," the names of actors that you think would be ideal for the roles, even if you think there is no way on earth that you will ever get them to participate. When asked to do that, I suggested some of the finest African American musical theater performers that I could think of (many of them Tony Award winners). Once again, if someone suggested that I dream big, I was ready to do just that! On my "wish list" were Tonya Pinkins, André De Shields, Larry Marshall, and the great and elegant singer Carl Anderson, a huge pop star who also loved working in the theater. When we finished the casting several weeks later, ALL of those actors had accepted roles in the show. The others may not have been on that initial list, but they should have been as they were equally wonderful, right down to all of the ensemble members. In addition to my fine collaborator Cheryl, the creative team included Mercedes Ellington as choreographer and the legendary, multi-award-winning, simply brilliant Luther Henderson as musical supervisor, arranger and orchestrator, and a fine group of designers. This was a true theatrical dream team that made the rehearsal period an experience that made us all "Jump for Joy" (another great Ellington song). Every day of those weeks of preparation for our opening was full of love, respect for the material and each other, passion, and a huge desire to serve both Shakespeare and Mr. Ellington well. When we reached that point in the process when we could do our first real run-through for ourselves and for the theater staff, there were several moments when I looked around the room and got a look back that said without words but quite clearly, this is something very special. This is going to work!

And it did. From our very first preview, audiences were rapturous and clearly taken with this combination of Shakespeare, the Duke and the stellar performances of this cast of heavy hitters. The Old Globe audience knew well the plot and characters of *Twelfth Night*, so they responded with "insider" knowledge when the Malvolio-based character appeared in his version of yellow stockings cross gartered, which became an outrageous lemon yellow-colored zoot suit in *Play On!* While being faithful to many of the particular characters of Shakespeare's play, for those in the know, Cheryl and I were careful to construct the musical so that it would stand on its own for those who did not know the source material as well. In this way the show attracted and appealed to the loyal Old Globe regulars but also drew in a new crowd of theatergoers who were more interested in the musical aspects of the show and the great songs of Mr. Ellington. Word spread quickly, and we were soon playing to sold out houses. The process up to this point culminated in a dream of an opening night with standing ovations, cheers for the company, champagne bottles popping and an announcement at the cast party that our enhancement producers were prepared to move the show to Broadway. In a word.... Bliss!

And those producers delivered on that promise. During the remainder of the run in San Diego, the money was raised and rave reviews from the local critics as well as good reports from "scouts" for the major theater owners in NYC helped us to secure a commitment for a house on Broadway. Ultimately we would land at the Brooks Atkinson Theatre, a beautiful and comfortable home for the show.

All things moved forward remarkably smoothly. At least to my knowledge they did, though there were discoveries on the business side that would later prove to be a hindrance.

With the original company intact, we went into rehearsal several months later making good changes based on things that we discovered during the run in San Diego and sorting out the comments that came to us along the way. Some very helpful and constructive, others completely ridiculous and quickly to pass in one ear and out the other. To admittedly name drop for a moment here, Bob Fosse once told me to find the patience and the strength to listen to everybody and to hear it all clearly and then have the good sense to know what you should quickly forget. Very good advice indeed. We did exactly that, and the show certainly kept getting better.

Previews were as ecstatic and as promising as they had been at the Old Globe. A well-known Broadway producer found me in the aisle at the end of a performance and said, "Well, this one will be your annuity. It's going to run for a long, long time." I don't pretend that it was everyone's cup of tea. What show is? But we were certainly finding an audience and making them happy and being true to our goals and our intentions, which in many ways is the best that you can do. We headed into our opening feeling very strong.

This all sounds wonderful and propitious, right? So why is the title *Play On!* not a more recognizable one in the canon of musical theater? It's because our run on Broadway was not a long one. We certainly got some absolute rave reviews from many critics but sadly not the rave that we needed from the *New York Times* (although even there we had very strong quotes). I discovered, too late in the game to do anything about it, alas, that the budget for the show was very tight, perhaps too tight, and that there was no reserve fund, which is needed with almost any show until it finds firm footing at the box office. That's certainly necessary when a show lacks big star names and a rock-solid rave from the *NY Times* (in my opinion it is wise to have that reserve fund even in that case). If you are lucky enough to get some good reviews and solid quotes, you also have to have the money to get those out there using all kinds of marketing tools. Mainly print and broadcast at that time (television commercials being especially helpful) and now through social media, which can be enormously effective with the right campaign. All of that requires dollars that we did not have. So despite ongoing, great audience reactions, a slow-but-too-slow build at the box office, and eventually several Tony Award nominations, we were not able to hold on during a busy season that was crowded with much bigger shows with larger budgets during award season. Other shows are spending bigger bucks to attract attention. Bigger bucks which were not available to promote our show.

However, we did once again have the saving grace of those Tony nominations. And the admiration of many who came to see the show during the Broadway run. In the latter category was Robert Falls, the artistic director of the renowned Goodman Theatre and a very gifted director as well. Happily he called several months later asking to include the show in the season at his theater in Chicago. That invitation turned into a co-production with Seattle Repertory Theatre, which was mounted with some of the Broadway cast involved as well as many of the creative staff. Once again, and in an odd way, the Broadway production served as the out-of-town tryout for this incarnation, and we were able to make further adjustments and finish some of the work that a constantly ticking clock may have kept us from getting to before opening night in NYC. As a result, the show opened in Chicago to truly rapturous reviews, including the most important one from the highly respected *Chicago Tribune* critic Richard Christiansen, who gave us a rave. The show set box office records in both cities. Later productions around the country produced quite similar results. As I write this, there is a plan in motion for a London revival. So clearly, we finally got it right. Perhaps a bit too late, in all honesty, but we finally got it right and finally produced the box office hit that the team of Shakespeare and Ellington most certainly deserved.

I faced a very big choice in the months after the show's opening when I returned to the Old Globe. The grant money that brought me to the theater, which had been extended for a second two-year stint, was now no longer available to support me or my position. The theater was willing to extend the strict confines of the budget to make it possible for me to stay (a small sum as a yearly salary but a very generous offer at the time). I was grateful for that. But I also felt that I had hit a quite tangible and unbreakable glass ceiling at the theater. Jack was not going anywhere; why would he? It occurred to me that I needed to. It was time for another one of those leaps of faith that I feel are so important in an artist's life. I took a very deep breath, said a little prayer, and I jumped.

Given the changes that quickly transpired over the next few months and the road that I would soon travel for the next long chapter of my life, everyone assumed that I had a place to jump to when I made the decision to leave the Globe. I did not. I just knew that the time had come to move on. Some of that choice was informed by the fact that I had started to do some television work, and there seemed to be the possibility that I might do more. But believe me, that was not guaranteed in any way. I contemplated going back to New York and in fact suspect that if other opportunities did not come knocking on my door that I would have done that. I suppose that would have meant getting back on the road as a freelance director and traveling from city to city once again and facing those bare white walls wherever I was working. Not such an appealing possibility, to be honest.

So it was quite a relief, both personally and professionally, when a number of things came together to put me on a road back to my hometown. Back to the city where my passion for the theater had been ignited so many years ago. And, rather amazingly, back to the theater where that fire in my soul had started to burn. I was going home in many ways. Though I was headed to the city where I was born and where I spent my early years, it was still a scary leap of faith. But I was very happy to be hometown bound, at least for the next few years.

Little did I know that going down that road would take me to my next artistic home for much longer than I anticipated. I certainly did not consider that when I packed up my life in San Diego, headed for the freeway, landed in Pasadena, California, and headed to a theater where Ethel Waters had dazzled me and planted a passion for the theater in my soul so many years before.

ACT VI, SCENE ONE

Setting My House on Fire

So that is how it happened. It was all of those long roads and many detours that brought me back to Pasadena Playhouse as artistic director. The journey along those roads begins to answer the question, "How did I get here?" The questions about how it happened are actually not nearly as important as the fact that it did happen. In 1997 I became the first Black person to lead a major theater in Southern California, and I was one of the few people of color in the country in this position. At certain times during my tenure I may in fact have been the ONLY one with that distinction. I felt bound and required to be successful. Not just for myself. I had to deliver in every possible way in order to prove that it was possible for a person of color to run such an institution successfully.

This was a tremendous extra burden to bear in a position that was already full of its own challenges and obstacles. But I had chosen to take it on, and now that I was here it was time for me to deliver. Whatever the highfalutin aspirations and movingly emotional aesthetic and social concepts an artistic director carries around in his or her being, finally, it is the work on the stage that must deliver and deliver strongly if in fact your intent is to build a great theater, as I proclaimed was my desire. As one of the first artists of color in this position, in the words of a song from *Hallelujah, Baby!* being good wasn't going to be good enough. Aiming for greatness was required as there were those who were there to support that goal, and there were others who most certainly were waiting for me to fail.

Here are some stories about choices that I made to "set my house on fire" and establish Pasadena Playhouse as one of the premier theaters in the country. That was my goal, and in pursuit of the goal there were certainly moments of greatness. I want to share with you some of the many productions that touched that holy grail for one reason or another.

The Real Thing

Anyone who knows me will tell you that I have a bit of a devilish streak. I admit it. Given my knowledge that there were many who thought that Pasadena Playhouse was doomed to suffer a Black Plague with me in place as artistic director, I decided to go about as far as I could in the other direction for the opening play of my first season. On a less devilish note, I also loved Tom Stoppard's brilliant, challenging and dazzling play *The Real Thing*. I chose this great play for all of those reasons to open the season, and I directed the production. This was about as polar opposite to expectations for the new guy as expectations could

The Playhouse I hoped to make great, 1997.

be. The play by the famous British author had an all–White cast for one thing and also a more sophisticated theatricality and dramaturgy than this theater had experienced in the recent past. Yes, I was indeed being slightly devilish in making this choice, but I was also making a point. I knew that I needed to prove myself in ways that were not required of other white artistic directors. I had to prove, and yes, I do mean prove, that I could do not just what they expected, which was work from the African American experience, but that I could do THEIR stuff as well and deliver that with equal style, wit, and theatrical panache. Thanks to the brilliance of this dazzling script, a wonderful first-rate cast and a fine design team we delivered the real thing for real! A new level of artistry on the stage of the theater was recognized right away and even better was celebrated immediately.

The *LA Times* critic, Laurie Winer at the time, wrote not just a rave review but the exact words that a new artistic director would want an audience to read: "A play of ideas passionately held and eloquently written from start to finish. 'The Real Thing' is the real thing, a play by a world-class writer, a play with insights that follow you out of the theater and deep into the night. Could this be a herald of a new and better age at The Playhouse? Epps' production is supple, smart and moving. He couldn't have picked a better debut vehicle for himself at The Playhouse."

Jeff Allin and Christina Haag in *Setting My House on Fire* with *The Real Thing* at Pasadena Playhouse, 1998 (photograph by Craig Schwartz Photography).

I don't think that I could have asked for a better critical response to introduce me and the kind of work that I hoped to do at the theater to the LA community. The naysayers were confronted not with my words but with those of this generous critic. Even better and just as much to be celebrated, the play was a huge box office success, reaching sales for a straight play that the theater had not seen for many seasons. Also, because the play deals with the challenges, travails, and emotional ups and downs of sustaining relationships at an early age (trying to find *The Real Thing*), it attracted a young audience to the theater in droves. With this production there was an exciting new energy at the theater, a new vitality, both on the stage and in the house. It declared, "Get ready for the ride!" boldly and proudly. That's what I hoped for. That was the standard that I hoped to set for the way the theater would move forward under my artistic leadership. This *Real Thing* was a real good way to begin that journey.

The Old Settler

The devilish part of me followed this up in a few months with a beautiful play called *The Old Settler* by John Henry Redwood. This play depicted the plight of a pair of near-middle-aged African American sisters living in Harlem as the older and more settled of the two, the more mature and levelheaded one, becomes romantically involved with a younger man. The play is rich in humor and in the end deeply touching. The sisters were brilliantly played by the divine combination of two of my favorite actresses: CCH Pounder and Jenifer Lewis. When I told a friend of this delicious casting, he raised his shoulders in anticipation and squealed "Oooh. Fire and ice, baby. Fire and Ice!" And indeed it was, as those two dynamic ladies who approached the work with such different tones and temperaments burned brightly on that stage at each performance. They brought not just their small apartment but the entire community of Harlem to life in a visceral and exciting way.

Word spread quickly, and my loyal brothers and sisters from the large African American community in LA heard the beat of the drum and made their way to Pasadena in droves. So happy to see a story on the stage of The Pasadena Playhouse that was from their history, that was from their culture, that was one of their stories. I was so pleased that they supported me and my greater ambition in this way. That certainly continued throughout my entire two decades at the theater.

Between the younger audience that rushed in to see *The Real Thing*, and the Black audience that took the A Train up to Harlem in Pasadena for *The Old Settler*, things changed very quickly, especially as newcomers in both groups returned to see much of the work throughout the season. I certainly recognized that the African American community was eager to support an arts institution which was bold and brave enough to have a Black person in a leadership position. The support from that community was steadfast, genuine and a great blessing. This was one of many reasons that it did not take very long before I was no longer the only person under 60 or the only person of color in the courtyard. This gave the theater a new life and a new vitality. And it gave me a great deal of pride.

A not-so-lovely offstage moment occurred around this time. Just to let you know exactly how bad things were at the beginning of my run. As we were going into production of this play, Lars Hansen, the executive director, came to me to discuss the artwork for the poster and the newspaper ads. He asked, shyly, but he asked if I thought that there was some way to depict the characters in the play as "neutral" racially. He wanted to know if I felt that it was really necessary to let the audience know that the sisters were African American. Of course, what he was really asking was if there was a way to hide the fact that the leading characters

Jenifer Lewis, one of my "old settlers" and me in 1998, Pasadena Playhouse (photograph by Craig Schwartz Photography).

are Black. Needless to say, I replied in the negative very strongly. I ridiculed the notion as both offensive and dramatically inept. While reacting with a good deal of passion, it did also occur to me that the request would only come from him as a result of pressure that he was feeling from the board, the community, some donors or all of the above about the sudden shift in the "complexion" of the work on the stage. I felt at that moment and for the rest of my years at the theater that celebration of the diversity of the work on our stage was the way to go and certainly central to our entire mission. Hiding what we were doing was wrongheaded, foolish and simply unacceptable. The eventual artwork for the show gratefully made it very clear that this was a tale of the experience of two African American women. This was the first of many battles over the years that had to be waged and hopefully won.

Play On! (In Pasadena This Time)

Things were going well, artistically speaking. Very well, in fact! After just a few seasons, the theater was indeed back in the game. Respected nationally once again, admired, desirable and very much a contender! This theater, though it had a long and venerable history, was not much in focus on the national scene when I arrived. That had changed rapidly, and we were the subject of articles in local and national publications, well respected by our colleague theaters who demonstrated those feelings by expressing their desire to work with us as co-producers and collaborators. Very quickly, I was frequently contacted by agents and commercial producers who wanted to discuss launching projects at The Playhouse. In short order that level of respect and admiration, which I hoped we would achieve, was very much in place.

However, even the most respected theaters can have financial challenges. The unspoken truth is that this is the case at one time or another at many of the most highly regarded theaters in America. Not-for-profit theaters like The Playhouse struggled constantly with an uneasy equation which balanced their budgets. This was a combination of earned income (box office sales) and contributed income which came from individuals, corporate support, and government sources. We were doing well with ticket sales, one production frequently surpassing the next. In fact, sales numbers had gotten so high that the problem came when we did not surpass total sales that just a few years ago would have been thought of as very satisfying. That was a measure of success, to be sure, but also a great challenge. The budget of any successful arts organization is a monster that constantly wants to be fed (much like that charmingly diabolical and voracious plant in *Little Shop of Horrors*). But on the whole, box office numbers were very strong. Where we were challenged was in increasing donated revenue. This had always been the case even before I arrived; it was the case now and in truth would continue to be a challenge in days and years ahead. But you see the challenge, and you press on to move on.

Frankly, I believe that one of the reasons donations were not higher was at least in part racially based. Though the theater was enjoying the much-desired artistic prestige that I'd hoped for and setting new box office records, the ugly truth was that there were still donors who were not so thrilled about a Black man being in charge. In fact, some felt that they were only biding their time until either they could get rid of me or until I ran away or until I simply failed in a spectacular way that would give them reason enough to push me out. They were going to have to wait for that which never happened. The unwillingness of some in the community who most certainly had the means to support the theater, even as they praised me and the work publicly, was a reality that we had to face. Now and then it was stated at a board meeting that we had gone too far with diversity. Or that there were too many people coming to the theater from beyond our immediate community. Too many outsiders (sadly, I kid you not). This was, of course, all easily decipherable code for "Maybe the theater has gotten too Black with 'you know who' in charge. We'll hold on to the big bucks until it belongs to us again." Shocking but true. But I was stubborn, perhaps a bit arrogant and not to be stopped. Remember, I was a man on a mission. If I was to be defeated, it was not going to be by small-minded people. Even rich, small-minded people. Keep your money; I'll find another way! (Did someone say arrogant?) And press on we did!

Offstage for another moment.... On reflection, I now think that I kept my personal reactions to the bigotry and racism that I often faced at the theater well buried. I'm sure that this was a defensive mechanism which kept it from hurting too much and also allowed me to keep going, putting mission above self. But the truth is, it still hurt. I was well aware of my privileged position as one of the few Black men or women in America leading a major arts institution and doing that with the aforementioned acknowledgment and praise of my peers and colleagues throughout the national theater community. But here at home base I was equally aware of smears, condemnations and slights that were entirely racially motivated. Though gratitude was expressed by board members and major donors in the community for my "saving the theater," I was hurt to realize how few times any of them extended invitations to their homes for dinners or holiday parties even when those invitations were extended to others on the staff. That kind of personal relationship with donors and board members was de rigueur for my White counterparts. It's not that I was eager to get into those big, fancy houses in Pasadena. I'd been in many big houses before, thanks very much. Actually I preferred to spend what little free time I had in the solitude of my own very lovely home. But the absence of those personal invitations along with the frequent not-so-whispered remarks, the furtive glances and the innate discomfort in conversations illuminated the ever-present "racial wall" that constantly set me at a distance. That was all palpable and painful.

Here's another example of the racial challenges that came my way. In my second or third year at the theater I was told by someone on the business staff that a subscriber had decided not to renew because I was programming too many Black plays, and he was fed up with it! The complaint, of course, came not directly to me but to others on the staff—white others—that in itself was somewhat racist. If you have a complaint about the programming, bring it to me. I'm capable of having rational conversations with you, so talk to me! I decided to press the issue and call the gentleman who was soon to exit the theater screaming and never to return again. I tracked down his number and made the call. "Hello, this is Sheldon Epps from Pasadena Playhouse." A now familiar pregnant pause. Finally, it is time for my line once again. "I understand that you are canceling your subscription because you feel that there are too many Black plays in the season. Is that right?" Another lengthy pause, and then to his credit a direct response, "Well, yes that is true. I think that you are overweighting the season with stuff that you like, that is not so great for all of us." A remark that was telling in so many ways. My line, "Well, the truth is that out of the six plays that we've announced for next year, only one of them could even broadly be described as a 'Black play.' If you are not willing to see even one out of six, then that really tells me how many you are willing and open to. So, I suppose that means that you'll have to find another theater that only does plays about people who look exactly like you if that is what you want." Clearly I was on a roll, but I stopped there. His reply, "Okay, wait just a minute.... Well, I guess ... Maybe ... Let me think about it." And the line went dead. Now this was only one of many conversations that I had like this because I heard the complaint somewhat frequently. And, in a twist that gives one hope, I must confess that there was a turnaround that surprised me. A few years later I was standing in our lobby at the end of a performance. A gentleman came over and said that he had to thank me. I asked him why. He reminded me of this conversation and told me that he was the subscriber on the other end of the call.

He then thanked me for sticking to my guns, for being willing to let him go, and most of all for persuading him to believe that he should broaden his theatergoing experiences and perhaps his overall point of view. He'd made the choice to keep coming and wanted me to know that he might have made a grave mistake if in fact he had canceled as he initially planned. He was grateful for the many seasons of good theater, for the stories and journeys that took him to different worlds, and most of all grateful that he got out of his own way! Hope springs eternal and sometimes brings great rewards. I am not one who requires a happy ending to every story, but I confess that I was grateful for this one.

Beyond sometimes responding boldly to criticism and risking the loss of a few closed-minded folks (and/or managing to open up a few minds), my most effective strategy was to keep working hard, to keep being bold and to surpass expectations. I knew that I had to overcome the expectations that I would surely fail or the expectation that any success that I had was merely a fluke rather than the product of hard work, theatrical intelligence and even business acumen. Surely my "lucky streak" would run out soon, they hoped. As with a great deal of racial prejudice, rising above biases, perceptions and expectations that were in place for "the other" was anathema to me and a real source of discomfort, consternation and even downright fear. Taking a cue from the divine and brilliant Toni Morrison, I decided that I would let racism be the racist's problem and not my own. But I do not deny that it was painful, both at the time and in memory.

Back onstage.... I felt that I could overcome all of that by burying my feelings and getting back to work! Given the difficulty with fundraising that continued to plague the theater, in my third year there we ran into a cash flow crisis. Once again, this was not unusual at an arts organization and not infrequent at this one. But it was serious and scary. There were many who suggested that the best way to deal with it was to cut back, to lower our artistic aspirations and perhaps care less about the quality of the work. Just stay alive. From my point of view there was no reason to stay alive at all if the quality of the work was poor. That was the state of the theater when I took the job, and we were not going back to that unfortunate aesthetic philosophy. If we were going to go down, let's go down gloriously. Let the ship sink not humbly and without notice but blazing with artistic pride and glory. Either way what you have is a ship that goes down. For me it was much preferable to exit in the latter fashion. And the possibility existed that a bold, attention-getting move might in fact right the ship and send it sailing forward rather than allowing it to sink.

Given all of this, I boldly proposed that the theater produce *Play On!* By this time, the show had been mounted at other major theaters including the Goodman Theatre in Chicago and Seattle Repertory Theatre with record-breaking success. But honestly it was still risky. It was a big show with all of the demands and complications of a major musical including cast size, big sets, musicians and even tap shoes! No doubt the budget for the show would be high, and that worried some. Many in fact. By this time Lars Hansen, who was really the one responsible for my "ascension to the throne," had left the theater. I suspect that he departed because he did not want to see the theater go down on his watch. He was no longer involved directly, but he was still connected to many on the board and the staff. He started a behind the scenes campaign to stop my madness, and I learned that he was broadcasting to anyone who would listen that I had only my own self-interest in mind and thought little of the health of the theater. Of course, exactly the opposite was true, but it sounded good to those who were inclined to listen and made those who were scared virtually terrified.

Sometimes those who serve in the position that I held just have to operate by their theatrical gut sense of what is going to work. And my gut was signaling strongly to me that this would be good for us. I was told by those on the staff (many of them using words from Lars) that I had "lost it" and that there was no way that the theater could even afford to do the show, so we could not go forward. I acknowledged that this was true, but rather than canceling I found a way to subsidize the production. My now-steady television career allowed me to loan the company some of the preproduction funding that was needed. I then convinced Arizona Theatre Company to co-produce with us, which meant that many of the production and rehearsal expenses would be shared, which represented a huge savings to the theater and at least lessened the risk, though it was not eliminated. But then risk ever is in Art!

We moved ahead with the co-production in place. I put together a cast of brilliant LA talent, and we had a joyous and thrilling rehearsal process. Even though it was all going wonderfully well, there is always the lingering, "Is this going to work?" question in the air, exacerbated by the theater's fiscal challenges in the weeks leading up to opening. Even as I languished comfortably in the brilliance of Ellington's music as it was deliciously delivered by these dazzling performers, there were images in my head of me crawling up the mast as the ship ablaze with fire was sinking. Yikes, talk about extra pressure!

With this frightening image strongly in mind but hopefully hidden from the acting company, we sailed forward joyously and smoothly and arrived at our first preview. As I hoped, the show was greeted with great enthusiasm immediately. Certainly comforting, but, once again, anything can happen. So we continued to work, polish and PRAY over the remaining previews. Given the enthusiastic audience reception and growing advance at the box office, I was not at all surprised that the reaction to the show on opening night was rapturous. The energy in the theater took off with the first sounds of the jazz band that accompanied the show and kept building throughout until a curtain call that shook the theater's very walls. I could not have been happier.

But even at the opening night festivities, there were knitted brows all around. Not from the company, of course, who could not have been happier or more proud. But from some on the staff and certainly from board members who knew how much was on the line. Had they been entertained? Most certainly. Did we all believe in the show? At this point, yes, we did. But lingering in the air was that all-important question: what would the critics say? This was still at a time when the largest newspaper in Los Angeles had real influence over box office sales, no matter how good word of mouth was. Our advance sales were good, but we still had a LOT of tickets to sell and big holes in the coffers that needed to be filled to keep us going throughout the current run with hopefully some to stash away for the rest of the season. Wrinkled brows abounded!

This was still a bit before the time when reviews would come out online before you saw them in the actual print publication. The anticipation over the *LA Times* review was great. Would the critic be as enthusiastic as our audiences? Even the placement of the review was a cause of concern. Where exactly would the critique land? Remember the theater is located in a film and TV land, and theater stories were often pushed to the back pages in the entertainment section of the paper, even when the reactions were enthusiastic. I hoped for placement at least on page two or three of the section.

When I got my hands on a copy of the paper in which the review was published, I quickly rushed to the Arts and Entertainment section, which on that day was much more important to me than national news, the stock market, local events or scores of the Dodger game. Lo and behold and praise the Lord!! The FRONT page of the entertainment section carried a huge production shot of the show "above the fold," taking up nearly half of the page and was followed by a review that one could honestly describe as a rave of raves. For the show, for the production, for the performers and for the good fortune of the theater to have this on our stage. The sun was shining, and the stars were bright!

This was followed over the next several days by equally enthusiastic reviews in publications large and small. The effect was activity at the box office that had not been experienced at the theater in many a season. We actually had to bring on extra staff to handle the demand for tickets, and the daily box office "wraps" were so high that people actually examined them carefully to make sure that another zero had not been added to the final total. This juggernaut brought to mind a famous *Variety* newspaper headline, "Boffo at the B. O.!"

Thank Heaven, my strong gut feeling had paid off. This was the first of many "saves" during my time at The Playhouse, and honestly, it felt damned good. Many of those who had expressed concern and doubt now boldly and graciously expressed gratitude and praise (alas, not Mr. Hansen who refused to believe that we had pulled it off). The ticket sales for the show gave us a chance to breathe freely for a while. The ship, either burning or barren, was not going down. The sails were full of the right kind of wind, and the current was strong. We could sail on happily for a while.

A much nicer offstage moment.... On the Monday of the final playing week of the run I got a call from a lovely gentleman named Jac Venza. He asked me if I knew who he was. I did indeed! He was the executive producer of many of the best performing arts productions to be found on PBS, which I had been watching since I was that theater-besotted high school kid. So yes, of course I knew who he was! Mr. Venza was known for producing televised versions of onstage performances with great class, skill, expertise and discriminating good taste. My new friend Jac, as he invited me to call him, said that he was in town for just a few days, and a friend who had seen the show early on insisted that he go to see it. He did, he loved it, and he was now proposing that we film the show at the theater to be broadcast as part of his most prestigious series *Great Performances.* He readily admitted that this was a crazy if not impossible task given that we only had one more week to run, but he was so enthusiastic about the show and Mr. Ellington's wonderful score that he wanted to try. Would I be all right with that? Let me think about it.... YEAH! Over the next hectic week we moved heaven and earth to put all things in place to make it happen. There was a lot to move and a lot to put in place including contracts for the theater, the acting company, musicians, the design staff and everyone on the television side as well. Somehow we got it all done and shot the show in the theater over the final weekend of performances and the following Monday. This produced a beautiful visual record of this miracle of a lifesaver for the theater (which looked incredible on camera, by the way). It was crazy to try to pull it off so quickly, but we did. There could not have been a more delicious cherry on the already delectable sundae of a show that was such a high point for me and for the theater.

Side Man

One of the great things about serving as an artistic director at a theater is that you certainly have every reason in the world to grow as an artist. I used to say that running a theater is like having a great kitchen where you get to prepare great meals to be consumed by your audience. But it is nice not to have to do all the cooking but to share the kitchen with other great chefs who hopefully whip up imaginative, tasty and rewarding dishes of their own. Both doing the cooking and watching the work of others that I admired helped me to grow as a director and as an artist.

However, in this position you are also a producer, and you frequently have to function well outside of the rehearsal room with equal strength, imagination and confidence. As a freelance director, you rarely have anything to do with the business side of the show. Your interest is and in fact should be entirely focused on "getting the show up" in the best possible way. But the producing side of artistic direction is very much involved in choosing and marketing a season, balancing a budget, negotiating contracts and securing rights for the work that is on the stage. The latter involves seduction, wooing, keeping your eyes and ears open and now and then even a little bit of larceny. That last quality did not come so easily for me on the business side of things. But I was learning.

Just a few months before needing to announce my fifth season at the theater I saw the Broadway production of a wonderful and moving play called *Side Man* by Warren Leight. The play justifiably won the

Tony and just about every other major award that season. I was smitten with the work and hoped to produce it at The Playhouse, but I suspected that would not be easy.

One of the challenges of running a theater in the greater LA area is that there were, at that time, three of us "Big Ones": Pasadena Playhouse, the Geffen and the almighty Center Theatre Group—truly the biggest of the big boys. CTG, as it is known, was founded by Gordon Davidson, one of the giants of the theater in Los Angeles and indeed of the national theater community. His accomplishments were legendary and worthy of the praise that he received from so many, including me. Gordon and I had a lovely relationship, and he always treated me with kindness, respect and even admiration. Though perhaps as an "up and comer" and not a true colleague initially. He was one of the first to greet me warmly when I took the job in Pasadena. Warm and gracious, yes, but there was no doubt, NO DOUBT that he was the Lord of the Manor in LA theater. Whatever Gordon wants, Gordon gets! That rule was not written down in any manual for new artistic directors in the area, but you soon learned that this maxim was kind of a rule not to be disobeyed!

Given its tremendous acclaim in NYC and at some other theaters, I wondered why *Side Man* had never been produced in the LA area. I assumed that either there was going to be a national touring production or that Gordon had the rights to do the play at CTG. A quick investigation told me that the former was the case; a major tour was being planned, so the rights were blocked in Southern California. Did I mention that part of the job was keeping your eyes and ears open? If not, let me say that once again. In short order I heard at a party that the planned national tour of *Side Man* was not going to take place and that subsequently the rights were going to be available for theaters to produce the play in the LA area. Armed with this unexpected news, I jumped out of bed early the next morning to make a phone call to the agent in charge of licensing the rights for the play. He thanked me for the call but said that the rights had probably been snapped up by Gordon for CTG. I told him that I suspected that might be true but asked him to please check. He called me back a few hours later (still quite early West Coast time, as I made my first call before dawn). He said that in fact the rights were available and that we would be able to produce the play. Something told me to use a cliché. "Could you put that in writing?" Surprisingly he said, "Sure." He would get something off to me right away. And indeed before the end of the business day, I had a written assurance that we had indeed been granted the rights to produce the play in our next season. Perfect!

Four or five days later a phone call comes in. The agent for the play is now calling me. He tells me that Gordon Davidson has contacted him about doing the play and is not happy to learn that we are about to announce it for our upcoming season. There is certainly no threat in his voice at all (that comes later), but certainly I am made aware that the power of the Lord of the Manor is being summoned to "persuade" me to accede to his desires. I suppose that in the moment I probably started shaking a bit, but something told me to stiffen the sinews and summon up my courage. I did and politely responded that I felt that we would be very, very happy to keep the play as a centerpiece of our upcoming season. And, by the way, many thanks for helping to make that happen.

There were many phone calls after that which included offers for other plays of the moment, the suggestion that we were being uncooperative at least and perhaps downright arrogant, and even veiled or not-so-veiled threats of some kind of legal action. By this point I was truly praising the gods for that one piece of paper that gave us the rights in writing. The people on the management side of the theater—ALL of them—suggest that we should back down and move on. I said no. Let's go to war. Let's fight. Tell them that if they sue, we will sue back and bravely drag it through court! We, of course, had none of the resources in place to make such a legal battle, but hey, it costs nothing to make a threatening response, right? And so we did. I never heard from Gordon directly, but I did receive gently persuading calls from members of his staff, cordially asking if I might reconsider. I dug my heels in and said a truly respectful NO.

Fortunately, if you look back through the archives of the theater, you will see that Pasadena Playhouse did in fact produce the West Coast premiere of *Side Man*. We produced the play, and gratefully we produced it well in a moving and striking production directed by Andy Robinson which was a huge success for us. Many of the reviews noted that it was noteworthy that this play was on the stage of The Playhouse rather than part of the season at the Mark Taper Forum, one of the CTG theaters. I agree. That was noteworthy indeed.

Shortly after this theatrical fracas I went to an opening at CTG. I saw Gordon across the room at the party that followed. My first instinct was to run and hide and hope that "Poppa Davidson" had not seen his churlish child. But we quickly locked eyes, and I stood my ground. He disengaged himself from the conversation he was having and headed my way with a somewhat inscrutable look on his face. Oy! Was I about to be ripped a new one by the paterfamilias of LA theater in front of our entire community? I steeled myself and prepared for the onslaught. It seemed that it took Gordon about half an hour to cross a rather intimate room as time went into slow motion. When he arrived, he put his arm around me in either a warm or an intimidating manner, I wasn't yet sure which, and he firmly guided me to a far corner of the room. When we arrived, he turned me squarely towards him and said, "Good for you. You fought for what you believe in, and you won. That's the way you have to play the game. Always fight for what you believe in! I'm pissed, but I am proud of you." Followed by the characteristic and genuinely warm Davidson squeeze of the shoulders. All slow motion ceased as he quickly walked away. I breathed for the first time since locking eyes with the great man. He was on the other side of the room before there was enough air in my lungs to acknowledge his gracious, respectful and heartfelt gift. His words meant so much to me and were both appreciated and inspiring. He let me know that I was playing with the Big Boys now and doing so skillfully and without intimidation.

The truth of those words stayed with me over many more years. Always fight for what you believe in. I did. At that time and for many more years to come as I continued to practice the fine art of artistic direction. Thank you, Gordon.

"Title—TBA"

There is no doubt that running a theater is truly rewarding in a number of ways. Especially if things are going well, if you can be proud of the work on your stage, and if that work is being admired and well received all around. But it is also tiring, sometimes frustrating, frequently exhausting and challenging for all kinds of reasons.

But now and then you get little gifts. That moment with Gordon Davidson was one. They can also come from friends, from the artists involved and from colleagues who push something your way unexpectedly that turns out to be rewarding. Fortunately that happened to me a number of times during my tenure. One of the best of those gifts involved a play whose title I shall reveal shortly. This is partially due to the fact that when the play first came to me, the front page said, "TITLE—TBA."

The name George Lane inspires a vast panoply of reactions from people in the theater business. In truth, invoking his name often causes people to shiver and tighten their shoulders. As the longtime head of the William Morris Agency Theater Department, he gained a reputation for being an incredibly tough (some would say intransigent) negotiator who was capable of reducing even the toughest people in the business to cries and whispers of terror. I personally never experienced "The Lane Treatment" at its worst, perhaps because I had known him for so long. I first met George during my time at The Production Company, the Off-Off-Broadway company that I built with my Carnegie schoolmates. I had a project that got some heat thanks to a favorable *NY Times* review, and I needed for the first time in my life representation as a director. Through mutual friends I had actually met the legendary agent Samuel (Biff) Liff who was at that time filling the position that later would belong to George as department head of the Morris agency. Biff kindly and honestly told me that he did not have time to help me but that he would hand everything over to his assistant named George. That began a long and cordial relationship with George during which he represented me as a director and later negotiated with me on behalf of his clients who worked at the theater. While I often found him tough and demanding, I sometimes would even say difficult, I never experienced the wrath of Lane that I heard about from others. I have a theory that even those who become the mightiest of the mighty tend not to pull out the diva behavior on those who knew them when. Now and then they may need a reminder about that ("Don't try it, girl; remember, I knew you when you were borrowing five dollars from me for a cup of soup." In my experience, that kind of read usually has a calming effect on a diva explosion). For whatever reason, George and I always had at the very least a respectful and collegial relationship, which was mutually appreciated.

So it was quite a pleasant surprise when George, now in his exalted position, called me and asked me to read a play that he represented. I was flattered, of course, and especially so when he told me the name of the well-known playwright. There were a couple of strings attached. George was upfront about the fact that the play was unfinished but told me that there was enough there to know what the writer intended. He suggested that I would want to grab it even in such an incomplete form. And that grabbing was a requirement. George posited the unusual requirement that I read the play within 22 hours after I got it and let him know yea or nay no more than two hours later. This meant that I had only one full day to read the play and decide whether or not it would receive one of the coveted slots in the season. That would be a VERY tight time frame for making such an important decision, especially when you're talking about new plays, which can actually be discussed and developed for years before they are deemed ready for full production.

I asked George why the parameters posited were so specific and required such haste. He told me that he was about to sign an agreement with Manhattan Theatre Club, one of the premiere theaters in New York City. If I agreed that this was a play of import and desirable for inclusion in our season, then he would "carve out" an exception in the agreement which would give Pasadena Playhouse the rights but prohibit any other productions of the play prior to it being produced at Manhattan Theatre Club.

Though this was all a bit mysterious and slightly cheeky behavior coming from George, I knew that we shared an astrological sign, so I also suspected that this was motivated by the "Scorpionic" mischievousness that we both were prone to. That made this even more intriguing. There was simply something enticing about the way that he talked about this play that encouraged me to believe that he was doing me a genuine favor by making this somewhat mysterious offer. My own triple Scorpio nature took over, and I said, "Send it."

Things got even crazier when I got the play. Besides the non-titled title page, the stack of papers was remarkably meager. I knew right away that George was absolutely correct that it would not take long to read it. The first scene of the play was pretty fully realized and very, very good (which is important because that is where an audience jumps on the train for the ride ... or not). However this was followed by several pages that simply said something like, "Scene to come. During this scene...." and then the writer went on to describe what would take place at this point in the action. This was enough for me to follow the action of the play, which in this form was absolutely fascinating and promising but hardly in any finished state. I was on the verge of putting the script down and calling George to say, "It's not the first of April, but this is a very good joke. There's no way in the world that I can give you an answer about this play based on what is here right now." And then

I turned the page. Thank goodness! Over the next several pages I was overwhelmed by a scene between the major character in the play and a new character who arrived in the action at the beginning of this scene. The exchange that took place between these two women (one Black and the other White) simply overwhelmed me. It was dramatically surprising and unexpected, driven by a combination of love, fury, fear, anxiety, intransigence and unexpected connection between two very disparate characters. When I finished that scene, I put the papers in my hand down beside me to catch my breath. Although I was alone in the room, I believe that I said out loud, "We've got to do this play!" I knew that if the playwright could come anywhere close to fulfilling the power of this extraordinary scene as he completed this play that it was going to be something of a masterpiece. My knowledge of the writer's previous work certainly gave me confidence that he could accomplish that feat, but what really pushed me to such an affirmative action, not to mention the quick phone call that I made to George, was the subject matter of the play and the visceral and profound power of this particular scene. Not to mention that feeling in the gut that I described before that sometimes makes a leap of faith entirely not just the right but the necessary thing to do. When I shared the news that I felt that we should include this play in our upcoming season and passed around the skeletal pages that led me to this decision, many of them thought that I had lost my mind. How could you commit to something that was so incomplete? Others thought that the subject matter was distasteful and not for our audience (if anything, the play addressed subjects that would soon be very much in the news on an all-too-frequent basis). I was told that it was reckless to want to move forward with the play. That, of course, only made my decision more firm (yes, a triple Scorpio).

Now all of this could have been disastrous. And looking at it from any logical point of view it was perhaps a bit reckless. One might use the word daring to put things in a more flattering light. I was just following my theatrical gut and an innate sense that this was a play that must be seen. Crazy? Perhaps. Reckless? I suppose. However, in every single way this turned out to be one of the best and most rewarding faith-filled leaps that I took over my two decades at the theater. No doubt about it!

As many of those reading this chapter and that last sentence may have already surmised, that play eventually was given the title *Doubt*, and the playwright is John Patrick Shanley. Gratefully George was entirely true to his word, and he made it possible for Pasadena Playhouse to include the play in our season. We took good care of this wonderful play and gave it a carefully modulated and thrilling production. The leading role, not so incidentally, was played by Academy Award winner Linda Hunt, who's portrayal of the tower-of-strength nun who displayed absolute certainty was powerful, slightly frightening, and very moving.

In another wonderful burst of good fortune, the Pulitzer Prize for drama was awarded shortly after the play opened at The Playhouse. For several weeks after this prestigious award rightly was bestowed on Shanley's masterpiece, the play could only be seen at two theaters anywhere in the world—Manhattan Theatre Club and The Pasadena Playhouse. As you might guess, trumpeting that news was a pretty strong instigator at the box office, and the production quickly sold out for the run and attracted newcomers to our theater in unexpected numbers. Particularly people from the film and television industry. The number of expensive black suits to be seen in the courtyard shot up suddenly. I am fairly sure that the theater and the city of Pasadena had not seen so many garments by Armani and Hugo Boss in its entire history.

By the way, when I read "that scene," I also remember thinking that these were the kind of roles and this was the kind of material that had the potential to prompt awards for the play and for the actresses who would be lucky enough to play the parts on Broadway. Shortly after the run of the play at our theater, that year's Tony Awards were presented for MTC's Broadway production of the play. And indeed *Doubt* received the award for Best Play, and Cherry Jones and Adrienne Lennox were awarded for Best Actress and Best Supporting Actress, respectively. I was not involved in that production, but I give myself a pat on the back for putting that out into the Universe!

In the months that followed, many other theaters across the country vied to get the rights to the play with the hopes of producing it months after it had been on our stage. I was asked over and over again how we got the rights to this award-winning play before everyone else outside of NYC. I certainly let the impression linger that it was due to a new prestige that the theater was enjoying under my tenure, a new level of respect in the field. Perhaps some of that is true. But I never shied away from telling the story that I have told here and letting people know that George Lane bestowed a gift on The Playhouse for reasons that I still don't know and cannot explain. But I was then and I am very grateful. No doubt.

Blue

Shortly after the birth of the new century I got a call from my dear friend and colleague Molly Smith, who was then serving as the artistic director of the esteemed Arena Stage theater in Washington, DC. She was calling me because she wanted me to read a new play called *Blue*, which was written by Charles Randolph-Wright. I was immediately charmed and taken with the play, especially because it reflected a great deal of my own family's background on my mother's side. Charles's semi-autobiographical play depicted the Clark family, who had achieved a level of success and fiscal comfort as the owners of the only Black funeral home in a small town in South Carolina. My mother's parents also were "well off," as folks in the town would say, because along with other businesses my grandfather acquired the funeral home which served the Black community in the small town of Windsor, North Carolina. Sadly, even the funeral homes were segregated—how odd that skin color dictated this separation of the races even after death. Especially as skin color disappeared as an issue and a reality pretty quickly after bodies were buried. Nevertheless, this racial stupidity was an ingrained reality, like many other things in the deep South for many decades. The play involved the Clark family's function and dysfunction over a number of years as issues from the past emerged and affected their complicated present. I thought the play was funny, charming, moving and for me personally attractive. I certainly knew these characters! After an equally funny and charming meeting with Charles, we decided to make this the first of what would become many collaborations over the next few years at several theaters around the country, in New York City, and at Pasadena Playhouse.

This first collaboration on *Blue* was blissful and productive. The rehearsal process at Arena Stage was a great delight largely because of the good work with Charles on the script that was delivered delightfully by a wonderful acting company headed by the fabulous Phylicia Rashad, who was ideal for the leading role of Peggy Clark. If the play was charming, and it was, the charm factor went up exponentially because of her sparkling presence, which brought a wonderful combination of a deft and light touch in the comic moments and a profound emotionality when the action of the play turned darker. Though we had met socially over the years, it was thrilling to work with her for the first time. Her cachet, still strongly intact from many years on a pretty well-known television show, and her much-hailed performance certainly were major factors in the tremendous success of the play's production at Arena Stage, where it was sold out for much of the run and extended at the end of its originally announced limited run.

A few months after the play had its grand finale at Arena Stage, we were invited to remount the production under the auspices of the Roundabout Theatre at their Off-Broadway space, which at that time was the intimate Gramercy Theatre on 23rd Street in Manhattan. This proved to be a lovely home for the production, which in addition to Phylicia included many from the DC cast, with the well-known actor Hill Harper assuming the leading male role (which was modeled more than a little bit on the idiosyncratic author of the play). The reviews were mixed, but mixed on the positive side, with praise once again for Phylicia, the acting company, and gratefully for the production. Positive quotes and excellent word of mouth propelled sales steadily over the run, and a *Variety* article focused on the phenomenon of a largely Black audience filling the Gramercy Theatre, which was a first for the Roundabout to be sure and a somewhat infrequent occurrence with an Off-Broadway show. The show buzzed happily along from spring and into summer of that year and had to close to open up the space for the next show in Roundabout's season. Plans were underway to move the play to a Broadway theater, and progress in that direction was positive. That is until the events of September 11 of that year, which rocked NYC, our country and indeed the entire world. Understandably the producers involved turned their focus to other things both professionally and personally. Certainly we were all understanding and disappointed but also grateful for the wonderful experiences we'd shared in the *Blue* world both in DC and NYC.

Fortunately the director of the play was also the artistic director of a theater in California. So he was able to initiate a further life for this play that he'd come to love and which he knew had been an audience favorite in both of the previous productions. Shortly we announced the play as part of the upcoming season at The Playhouse and also arranged for a national tour which included several other major theaters from one side of the country to the other. Based on that gut feeling once again, I knew that the play would work in my theater, but two very lucky pieces fell into place of what is always a puzzle, even with the most surefire of productions.

First of all, a sudden, unexpected opening in Phylicia Rashad's schedule made it possible for her to repeat her great performance at my home base theater. As her character in the play frequently intoned, "Divine." That alone was a fairly major guarantee of success for The Playhouse incarnation. I was thrilled to take this journey with her once again in my artistic home.

But a completely surprising turn of events guaranteed that the charm and excitement quotient of this incarnation of the play was about to shoot up unexpectedly.

Through a number of contacts, Charles was able to be in touch with a true show business legend. To be honest, I didn't think that we had a shot in hell of making this proposed casting a reality when he first told me the news. I have rarely been flabbergasted by anything. But I confess that I was when a rep for this icon told me that she wanted to have lunch with me to discuss a smaller but dynamic role in the play, the character of Tilly Clark, mother-in-law to Phylicia's character. I met this Divine One at a chic Chinese restaurant on the ground floor of her apartment building in Beverly Hills. As I sat there, having arrived incredibly early to make a good impression, I saw her coming around the corner in her Rolls Royce, heading into the building garage on the lower floor. Talk about chic! In a few

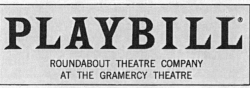

Blue... **Off Broadway at the Roundabout The-atre, New York City, 2001.**

minutes she arrived, definitely changing the temperature in the room as she carried in the kind of aural light that surrounds those with true star quality. We talked for a blissful hour and a half. When she stood to leave, she stopped suddenly and said, "Oh, can I ask you one more question?" I would have been quite happy to answer another hundred if she so desired, so I answered simply, "Anything." Well, I was flabbergasted once again when she said quite simply and definitively, "When do we start?" It was only at that moment that I truly believed that the role of Tilly in The Pasadena Playhouse production of *Blue* would be played by the legendary Miss Diahann Carroll.

That's right, Miss Diahann Carroll! She who was not only one of the great beauties of our time but also a trailblazer in almost every area of show business lore, including movies, television, cabaret and Broadway theater where she made history as the first Black woman to win a Tony Award as best actress in *No Strings*. That was even before her history-making role as the eponymous character in the history-making television series "Julia," which I used to watch with my parents, both of whom adored her, just as I did. That Diahann Carroll! I repeated that phrase several times as I drove back to Pasadena. And I almost ran off the road when I actually realized that Diahann Carroll and Phylicia Rashad would be appearing on the stage in a Pasadena Playhouse production AT THE SAME TIME!

This excited me for a number of reasons. All of them guaranteed to equally excite the LA theater audience and to make national news, which it surely did! With all of the great success that we'd had with the play in the previous productions, I knew that this casting would lift the experience to an even higher level. The star quotient only got higher and more stellar when the talented and incredibly handsome Clifton Davis agreed to join the company, playing Diahann's cherished son and Phylicia's long-suffering husband. Needless to say, tickets began to fly out the door as soon as this illustrious company was announced. The clamor for tickets lasted throughout the entire run.

The rehearsal process was delightful. How could it not be with these two spectacular ladies leading the company. Believe me, here were two dames who knew how to truly LEAD a company through the creative process, and they both did exactly that with their distinct charm, style and amazingly good humor day by day by day. Now and then I had to pinch myself to be sure that working through a scene with both of them in place was not a fantasy but actually my current reality.

Occasionally, I had a particular challenge in keeping my focus on the play during rehearsals as I was a very willing audience for Diahann's stories, both personal and professional. And there were plenty of them. After one particularly revealing tale about one of the attention-getting men in her life, I asked her if she ever thought about writing a book. She said, "Actually I did write one. But you are right, I should do another one and tell the truth this time." She did exactly that, and her second, much-more-candid memoir became a best seller and was quite the delicious read. I still cherish my signed copy.

I was not at all surprised but certainly thrilled to know that the play charmed audiences once again, and the stunning combination of Miss Carroll and Miss Rashad was celebrated at every performance. We once again had record-breaking sales at the theater for a straight play. Even during a week when Phylicia had a previous commitment and had to miss several performances, we were nearly sold out for every show. No doubt, this was because I called on an old friend to replace Phylicia for that week, and she graciously accepted. There was no disappointment at all during those performances as those audiences had the pleasure of seeing the equally dazzling combination of Miss Carroll and Leslie Uggams. Leslie brought her own distinct class, star quality and panache to the role and was so successful in the part that we asked her to take the play on the national tour that traveled from one coast to the other for several months.

Over the years since we started this journey at Arena Stage in DC, the play has been produced frequently around the country. It was recently announced that the play will have an upcoming revival in NYC under the auspices of the Apollo Theatre. Two of my original ladies will be involved, as the production will be directed by Phylicia Rashad, and the role of Tilly will be in the very sure hands of Leslie Uggams. Will theatrical wonders never cease?!?

Once again, the color BLUE had served me well.

Hitmaker

The problem of having hits at a theater company is that everyone wants you to keep having hits. It's never quite clear to me why people think that this minor miracle is so easily accomplished, but they do! While that is quite flattering in one way, success breeds its own monster, and you are expected to top yourself every time you go to bat. It becomes an inspiring challenge, yes. Especially in a regional theater, as these companies were founded to get away from the hit-making mentality of the commercial theater world. Alas, no one seems to have explained that very well to the boards of directors of our theaters. Or they find ways to conveniently forget that box office returns and record-breaking sales are not the only measure of a theater company's success. Especially as performing arts organizations have become more and more dependent on ticket sales as a part of the overall budget, as government grants vastly decreased and foundation grants diminished and as boards avoided their primary responsibility, which is raising money to support the organization, the desire and necessity to focus on making hits time after time became more and more prevalent.

They loved you for being a great artist, but in truth they love you a lot more if you are also a hitmaker. I personally have nothing against producing work that draws a big audience. This means that the work is connecting with audiences to such a degree that people go out and tell others to see it. Ultimately the best sales tool in the theater is word of mouth. But it becomes a great challenge and something of a burden when as soon as you break one record the expectation is that you will find a way to do it again next season. Or sooner if possible. I say with both pride and frankly a degree of consternation that I found ways to do that. Perhaps more often than I should have. With some ambivalence I offer you here a few more tales of when and how we were able to make hits happen.

Fences

Among producers of film and theater projects, there is an often used manipulation, to put it kindly, that has often been deployed to attract well-known artists to a project. That is the "Well, he told me that he'll do it if you'll do it" gambit. I confess that I used this bit of producorial trickery to attract an amazing cast to my production of the great play *Fences* by August Wilson.

I had long admired this play, ever since I saw the original production on Broadway that was directed by Lloyd Richards (and he actually did get the prize in this case, winning the Tony Award as best director that year) and starring the legendary James Earl Jones as Troy with the less-well-known but equally brilliant Mary Alice as a long-suffering but ultimately triumphant wife. Of all of August Wilson's great work, this is the play that I most admired and knew that I wanted to get to one day as a director. A sudden hole in our season sent me running out to secure the rights to the play, which involved getting approval from the estate for me to direct. A bit of a challenge, but one that was met. We got the approval to go ahead with the production. While any production of this classic American work is cause for anticipation, I did want to make it special if I could. Remembering the original Broadway production which had reached an iconic status in the minds of those who saw it (and even in the minds of those who hadn't) provided both a sense of slight intimidation about approaching this work but also a push to make it something that would be noteworthy both locally and hopefully nationally.

I knew that Laurence Fishburne was in LA doing a play at the Mark Taper Forum. Through a good mutual friend I had also met and spent some time with Angela Bassett. By now you can see where this is going. I went to Angela first and perhaps indicated with more confidence than I had any right to that I believed that I could get Laurence to do the play if she would do it. Angela told me that she loved the play and the role and that if Laurence would do it, she would do it.

So… Of course it was time to get to Laurence. I suspected that he might not want to do a play again quite so quickly after his current run. But I also knew that he greatly respected the work of Mr. Wilson. I took the leap of faith once again. I instructed my assistant to make the trip downtown to the LA Music Center an hour before an evening performance and wait by the stage door for Laurence to arrive. He was to give him a handwritten note from me, telling him how much I wanted him to do the play and that in fact I was sure that Angela Bassett would do it if he would do it! He was not to return to the office until this note was actually in Laurence's hands directly, even if this meant that he had to spend the night on the steps of the stage door waiting for the next subsequent performance. The combination of a tenacious assistant and good timing allowed him to sleep in his own bed as he was able to hand the note to Laurence as he entered the theater that night. I knew that it was important to get to Laurence directly rather than going through agents or managers, who would not be thrilled that he was being asked to work for a not-for-profit theater salary once again rather than the bountiful bucks that he was making for movies at the time. I had learned that the best strategy was to get the actor excited and captured by a notion before that fiscal conversation could happen. I prayed that he would be enticed by this great play, by the phenomenal role, and by the opportunity to work with a beautiful and great leading lady with whom he had shared tremendous success already in the film *What's Love Got to Do with It.*

Even with all of these "right" elements in place, I was honestly doubtful that it would happen. I spent the night thinking about ways to hold on to Angela when her preferred leading man declined, hoping that she would still do the play with someone else. But early the next morning, just as I got into my office, the phone rang. It was Laurence. He thanked me for my note and … wait for it … invited me downtown to see the play that he was doing so that we could meet after and discuss working together on this masterpiece. Obviously I canceled any other plans, and I was at the Mark Taper Forum several hours later.

Laurence, of course, was wonderful. Not a very good play, nor up to his very special gifts as an incredible stage actor, but he was wonderful. When we met after the performance, he was gracious, welcoming, enthusiastic and ready to go. It was actually me who posed the question of whether or not "his people" would be all right with his committing to doing another play quite so quickly. (We were going into rehearsal just a few weeks after the current run finished.) Would they let him do that? His voice fell into a basso profundo range that I would come to know well as he said, "They don't 'let me' do anything. I tell them what I 'want' to do and they make it possible. Sometimes things are just right and you have to do what you have to do to make them happen." I did not argue. Just a few days later, both Laurence and Angela were signed, sealed and delivered, and we announced that this dynamic team would bring this great play to life on our stage. The entire run sold out very quickly.

With those two in place in the leading roles, it was easy to fill out the rest of the company with an illustrious group of actors, all of whom had a good deal of recognition and audience appeal on their own. Actors were eager to be a part of a production of this great play and especially so with these two great actors in the leading roles. Ultimately the cast included Wendell Pierce, Orlando Jones, Kadeem Hardison, and a young "find" named Brian Terrell Clark in the role of the troubled son. With all of those names in the cast, it was easy to make the production a box office hit. The bigger challenge was living up to the high expectations that quickly emerged. But we did. The potential for this to be a very distinctive and special production that would rival the memories of the Broadway original cast was apparent from the first day of rehearsal (which ironically was the first of August). I will always remember Laurence setting a tone and a high mark for excellence with his reading of his very first line of the play, which sent electricity through the room and immediately gave everyone else a standard to aim for, which they all did with brilliance. Our weeks of rehearsal were joyful and fun-filled but also full of an "electrified tension" that was brought on by the demands of the play, the personalities of the actors involved, their previous history together and everyone's desire to "deliver" in honor of August Wilson. This admirably fraught rehearsal period led us to an absolutely electric opening night when the last line and the fade out on the play was met with the kind of earth-shattering audience reaction that had us all wondering if Southern California was experiencing one of its not-infrequent earthquakes. It was a theater-rocking, seismic moment to sure. But it was not brought on by nature but by artists delivering a great piece of dramatic literature with earth-shaking power, sensitivity and humanity that was palpable to all in the house. Sometimes, thank the Lawd, you just get it right! This time we did. We started, of course, well ahead of the game given the brilliance of this wonderful play by August Wilson. The homespun but eloquent words of the play provided inspiration and great passion to this fine acting company led by Laurence and Angela. The result represented real artistry by these Black artists. Real Black Excellence on display. It rarely got any better than this.

The news of this astounding event traveled quickly. As we were almost completely sold out even before the play opened even with an announced extension, we spent the next four weeks wrangling over house seats, those few remaining seats that you hold back for last-minute emergencies. Well-known names from every area—entertainment, politics, social causes, and government dignitaries—were coming out from all over the city, the country and in fact from all over the world, all clamoring to see the production. The staff of the theater spent most of the day figuring out how to fill house seat requests from yet another movie star, yet another mayor, or yet another dignitary from the London theater all calling (usually at the very last minute) and all saying that they just had to see the play. The jockeying for those last few seats was fierce each and every day of the run.

Not surprisingly some of that clamoring for seats came from producers from NYC, both from the not-for-profit and the commercial side. The starry pair and the incredibly positive reviews for the production quickly caught the attention of what I call "the shoppers," those producers in Manhattan who keep a sharp eye on what is going on at regional theaters (especially when stars are involved) with the hope of bringing notable productions to the east coast. I heard from many of them who quickly became competitive in their offers to transfer the production to Broadway. Either for a limited run or an open-ended one. Sadly, despite initial representations to the contrary, it turned out that the rights were entangled by someone who already had an eye on doing this (but never did!), and, despite my pleas to work in collaboration with that person, their ego kicked in and we were not allowed to pursue all of the opportunities that we had to move the production to NYC. A few years later, there was a very praiseworthy production of the play starring Denzel Washington and Viola Davis, which was also hugely successful and award winning and led to a very fine film version of the play. I confess that I had a combination of sadness and some joy when colleagues who saw that production on Broadway would call me after and say, "Yeah, it was really good.... But not as good as yours." Ahh, Fate!

But I am content with having hit a home run with our production of *Fences*. I know, to extend that metaphor just a little bit further, that we knocked it out of the park! Watching the high level of artistry that was on the stage at every performance and seeing the audience connect with the actors in a visceral way and exploding with appreciation at every curtain call was incredibly gratifying. It was a huge box office success, the highest-selling production of a straight play up until that time in the theater's history. But it was inarguably a huge artistic triumph as well. If my goal from those early years was to make a great theater in

Pasadena, surely during the run of this great play with this inspired cast that goal was fulfilled. For these shining moments we certainly enjoyed greatness.

Offstage once again ... just after we announced our production of *Fences* (even before the sly manipulations that blessed us with the two attention-grabbing stars who would lead the company) a lovely woman named Lesley Brander who worked in our fundraising department asked to come to my office to discuss a new idea for bringing contributed resources to our theater. Lesley made her case by opening with this line: "Have you noticed that many of the most popular productions that we have on the stage are those which attract African Americans and other people of color? And, as a result, have you noticed that foundations have provided us with generous grants because we are doing that work and literally changing the face and complexion of this theater, both onstage and off?" I replied that this had not completely escaped me. "Well, don't you think that we should do something about that?" I asked her what she had in mind.

Lesley, who would certainly be described as an out-of-the-box thinker, both as a fundraiser and as a woman, then laid out her vision of what she wanted to call the "Sheldon Epps Theatrical Diversity Project." Many fundraising initiatives are put in place to get something started or to get something going. In this case, Lesley was suggesting that we create a fundraising drive that would reward something that was already happening and already going very well. Her strong feeling was that there were many donors, especially well-to-do African American donors in Pasadena and the greater LA community that would be willing to support the theater not just by buying tickets but with their donated dollars as well. I was immediately on board with her overall idea about this but not so much taken with having my name in first position. I truly was hesitant about that, and she was truly insistent and wore me down. She argued, correctly as it turned out, that there were many who wanted specifically to support my efforts in this vital area of diversity and wanted to validate the fact that this had been a mission, a fight, and indeed an achievement for the theater primarily because a person of color was the artistic director. Even more because this particular person of color was in that position. In truth, I am not quite sure that I ever said yes to this naming aspect, though I certainly endorsed her idea, but it was not long before that appellation was out in public. Quite quickly the first fundraising gala for the "Sheldon Epps Theatrical Diversity

Project" was announced to take place on Opening Night of *Fences*. And shortly after that the event was sold out and had many sponsors and generous patrons in place. Over the next several years the Diversity Project became one of the most successful fundraising instruments that the theater enjoyed. Unlike me, who only had questions about the naming but endorsed the idea overall, there were those who questioned and in fact vilified the idea that we would make a lot of noise about our success in this area. They thought that it was a terrible idea that was bound to hurt us eventually. Those naysayers were served and made to eat quite a lot of crow over the next several seasons. Over time, perhaps begrudgingly through crow-stuffed mouths,

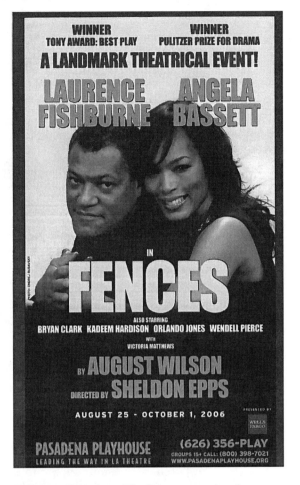

Fences at Pasadena Playhouse, starring Laurence Fishburne and Angela Bassett, 2006.

many of them expressed their gratitude for the thousands of dollars that rolled into the theater's accounts which helped to support all of our work for many seasons. We had many more opening night galas celebrating the work of artists of all colors. Many never admitted that they were wrong. But the proof was in the tasty and advantageous pudding that helped to keep the theater afloat for many seasons.

A more personal but equally important offstage moment … Lesley, that lovely, tenacious, forward-thinking, sometimes aggravating but always incredibly supportive woman who pushed this idea up the hill with such great energy and success would later become my wife. She would spend many more years convincing me of all kinds of things and winning many battles. I would say almost ALL of them. I have sometimes been beaten and bowed, I confess. But I have always been grateful and always lifted up by her great love and devotion to me. That has been and still is a great part of both my personal and my theatrical success. She has often pointed me in the RIGHT directions and frequently pushed me to be brave enough to go down the challenging but "right" roads, even when those directions were a bit frightening. My gratitude for all of that is ineffable.

Sister Act

If you are lucky as an artistic director and if your theater company is enjoying respect and admiration in the field, you have the good fortune to have people proposing many good projects for inclusion in your season. You spend a great deal of time meeting with directors, actors, playwrights, agents and managers who have ideas for both new work and revivals. As you might suspect, some of these ideas are very good, some merit attention and thought, and quite truthfully, now and then you leave such a meeting wondering, "Why would anyone want to do that?" But it is a wide range of taste and ideas that makes for exciting theater. And sometimes the craziest ideas turn out to be quite successful.

The process of selecting the season usually involves keeping eyes and ears open for the good projects, thinking through those that you believe have potential and combining those good notions with your own thoughts about titles or playwrights that you believe the theater should get to at some point. In this busy mix, now and then you even get to think about those plays and musicals that you're personally attracted to as a director. And fortunately, in the midst of all of the other responsibilities you must fulfill, you actually do get to direct. How nice to be able to give oneself a job, doing exactly what you want to do. All of this involves a good deal of rumination and contemplation that pretty much goes on perpetually all year long. Most of your choices are usually made quite slowly and deliberately over a long period of time as things go on and off of the schedule, sometimes to return in a later season, and frequently never to be thought of again. On some very, very rare occasions

I said yes right away! But not very often.... I can probably count the number of times that this happened over 20 years on one hand.

But it certainly happened with swiftness and sureness actually during a meeting with a fine gentleman of the theater named Peter Schneider, and with very satisfying results. Peter had a very long history in the theater, one that was similar to my own, as he started his career doing a wide variety of jobs in Off-Broadway and regional theaters. After many years of toiling happily but without great remuneration, I suspect, his steadfast devotion to our artform led to his illustrious position as head of Disney Animation and their subsequent Theatre Division from which came such huge successes as *Beauty and the Beast* and *The Lion King*, the former hugely successful and the latter one of the biggest hits ever! After many years on the producing side of things, Peter was eager to continue his ongoing life in the theater as a director. He took me to coffee one day and said, "I've secured the rights to the film *Sister Act*, and I want to do it as a stage version. I'm hoping that you'll be interested and that we can start the project on the stage of The Playhouse." I suspect that he actually did not complete all of that last sentence as I believe I jumped excitedly in and said YES shortly after the word "interested," or perhaps it was "start." I don't remember which, but I do know that I said yes to this perhaps more quickly than I had given a positive answer to anything else. Peter, I think, was a bit startled by the swiftness of my response, especially as I started to discuss scheduling with him right away. I wanted to give him and the collaborators involved all of the time that they needed, but I also wanted to include this in our season as soon as they felt ready to go.

That getting ready to go involved some careful decisions, particularly in the area of the music for this new stage version. There were subsequently many debates about whether the show would use the music from the film version or if a new score would be created. People came down on both sides of this, and I recall that we went back and forth on what was the best way to go. However, when Peter told me that he felt that he could persuade Alan Menken to do the score, for me the debate was pretty much resolved. Peter knew Alan well from his work at Disney in addition to his other terrific theater work, including *Little Shop of Horrors*. Peter had in fact been the company manager for the original Off-Broadway production many years before. How constantly history brings our lives back together in the theater. They decided on a young but quite brilliant lyricist named Glenn Slater to put words to Alan's music. Cheri and Bill Steinkellner would adapt the original movie script for the stage. With this team in place for what was already an exciting idea, I was quickly able to persuade Susan Booth, artistic director of the Alliance Theatre in Atlanta, to join us as our co-producing partner.

After several months of readings and workshops, the show arrived on the stage of The Playhouse. Every production that is good creates a certain kind of excitement and energy in a theater, whether it is Shakespeare, Rodgers and Hammerstein, Noël Coward, August Wilson, or Cole Porter. But I think that there is always something special and distinctive about the energy that bursts off the stage of a world premiere when it is actually working. And this *Sister* was working in a heavenly way. Whatever issues the show had at its first performances, and every new musical has issues, it immediately jumped off the stage and into the hearts of our audiences and was embraced warmly and enthusiastically like an old friend in a brand-new suit. Peter and company were in rehearsal for this show during the phenomenally successful run of *Fences* on our stage. He humorously but pointedly made a sly comment one day about how the heat was on because of "Your goddamn hit!" referencing the pressure his show was under as it would be following the juggernaut that was my blissfully star-studded production of the Wilson play. But it was clear from the first preview that he had a goddamn hit of his own and that the theater blissfully could enjoy back-to-back juggernauts. What a one-two punch this was! The record-breaking success that *Fences* enjoyed as a play was now matched by *Sister Act* becoming the best-selling musical in Pasadena Playhouse history. The Alliance Theatre enjoyed equal success when the show transferred to Atlanta. It was wonderful to see the production there and to note the changes that had been made (all to the better) based on what the team had learned during the Pasadena run. Shortly after the opening in California, the buzz began and this *Sister* started a long-but-sure journey to Broadway.

All kinds of things can and do happen along that road. The truth is that the originating producers (in this case Pasadena Playhouse and Alliance Theatre) often have little to do with the fate and development of a show once it leaves our stages. At some point the decision was made to replace Peter as director on the show. The very skilled Jerry Zaks came aboard to helm the show, along with other changes that were made during a somewhat circuitous path that eventually led to Broadway, including productions in major European cities and on the West

End. But eventually it did land on Broadway where it had a long and successful run followed by national tours and numerous productions all over the world. Over the years I have been surprised and thrilled to read about productions on almost every single continent ... at least the ones that are not completely frozen!

A great side benefit of all of this was ongoing support to our theater. As one of the originating theaters that produced the show, we shared a small percentage of revenue from the commercial productions for many years. While the checks that we received were nothing like those thrown off from *A Chorus Line* or *Hamilton*, they did represent a nice, healthy income stream which supported many other projects for The Playhouse over the next several years; big or small, those checks were always greatly appreciated.

All of this the result of a coffee meeting and one of the fastest yeses I ever uttered. Once again that gut feeling served the theater well. There is no doubt that deep thinking and careful contemplation are great tools, and deep consideration is necessary and required most of the time. But now and then acting quickly from a strong instinct can have all kinds of rewards. Given the specific case of this tale of spiritually awakened nuns who learn to lift their voices in secular, theatrical and spiritual ways, now and then those rewards can even be heavenly! We were all very grateful to that soulful *Sister.*

So even with ambivalent feelings, I was certainly happy to be a hitmaker during this period. The productions of *Fences* and *Sister Act* came back-to-back at the end of the same season. Both broke box office records, filled the house and the theater's bank account and displayed admirable theatrical diversity, skill and genuine artistry. Though I may have sometimes resented having to be a hitmaker, I was certainly proud and happy when I felt that the work was artistically worthy of that designation based on merit. So many of the hopes and dreams that I had for the theater were coming true. And not just in my imagination. We were truly hitting that standard of greatness that I hoped for when I accepted the job. Life at the theater was full of joy and bright with possibilities.

And then, the lights went out....

A Dark Chapter

The first decade of my time at the theater was full of wonderful accomplishments and the expected but frequently surprising highs and lows that are inevitable in the life of a theater. There were fortunately lots of highs and substantial changes for the better, both onstage and off over those first ten years. We had certainly regained the much-desired national reputation for excellence and diversity that was envied by many. Then quite suddenly, while riding the crest of this good wave, like many other performing arts organizations we were hit hard by the national economic downturn in 2008 that was brought on by evil economic forces which even now I don't begin to understand. But I know they hit us hard. Especially the stock market crash, which gave donors an easy out when it came to responding to our sincere requests for donated revenue and support. It became an "easy pass" for many of those well-heeled doors to tell me and those who worked in the development department that they "simply could not make a donation this year as they had been hard hit by the recent events, and their portfolios were down by 25 or 30 percent." I suppose it never occurred to them to realize that I actually realized that this meant that the poor buggers were down to a net worth of only $30,000,000 or $40,000,000 (or more). However were they managing to get by? My noting that to them, dripping with false sincerity and a good dose of sarcasm was probably not exactly the right way to go. But I also knew that there was very little that I or anyone could do to loosen up the purse strings during that time. My conversations with the leaders of other theaters made it clear that this challenge was hitting all of us.

In the case of Pasadena Playhouse, this exacerbated a situation which had plagued the theater for many years. A deal was struck many years after the reopening intended to sever the entanglement between the theater professionals who were running the place and the more business-minded forces who were still involved with the company. That deal was not a good one for the theater. In order to cleanly separate the two a not-for-profit-producing organization was formed to manage the theater on behalf of the city. Sadly, that deal included the new not-for-profit inheriting existing debts. This placed a very large-sized monkey on the new producing company's back. Not the best way to begin. Anyone reading this who is planning to start a theater, a dance company or an opera company should take my advice and try to do that without beginning your life with an existing debt load.

And so the double whammy of this ongoing debt service and the wallop of the 2008 economic downturn was a gut punch which really rocked the theater's world. Running a theater company is never easy, but this was quite a one-two punch. Perhaps not exactly a knockout punch, as we kept going, but there is no doubt that we were reeling around the ring in a pretty significant daze! I described this time with the image of someone running down a mountain who looks over their shoulder to see a large snowball in the distance behind them and knowing that it is most definitely headed in their direction. The running gets faster, but so does the snowball. And bigger! It's not very long before you find yourself looking over your shoulder at a huge mountain of snow that is either an enormous ball or perhaps an avalanche. Frankly, it does not matter which. If you don't keep running fast enough, you will most certainly be consumed by this wall of white at any moment! Not a fun way to run a theater and not a fun way to live!

This was especially perplexing and frustrating as on the other side, artistically, things were still going well. At a time when selling theater tickets seemed to have been declared illegal at most companies all over the country and even on Broadway, we set yet another new box office record for the theater with a show called *Stormy Weather* starring my old friend Leslie Uggams, playing the great legend Lena Horne. A pretty tasty combination that was reflected in record-breaking ticket sales. It was very odd to have such a huge hit on our hands and to look over our shoulder to see that fast-traveling deficit avalanche ever approaching and growing larger. During that same season we also had highly praised and hugely successful productions of Lillian Hellman's *The Little Foxes* and *Crowns* by Regina Taylor. And even a new musical called *Baby It's You!* that would wind up on Broadway the following year following the successful run at The Playhouse. We were, even with the challenges, artistically bright and shining, still displaying exactly the kind of artistry and diversity that I so cherished for the theater. But the snowball kept getting bigger and bigger, and the running was getting harder and harder. Something had to give.

A new executive director named Stephen Eich arrived on the scene around that time. He had a track record that was highly respected having worked at such well-regarded theaters as Steppenwolf in Chicago and the Geffen Playhouse on the opposite side of Los Angeles (same city, but a world away in so many ways). I admired his experience and knowledge; though, to my mind, he was not fully invested in the company—which would sadly prove true eventually. But he was smart and knew the territory. Stephen was also maddeningly blunt. Often brutally so. Shortly after his arrival and having had a short period of observing the running game and being drawn into it like all of the rest of us, he came to me with his accustomed blunt and brutal assessment. He said, "We've got to shut it down!"

After over ten challenging but rewarding years of building and sustaining the theater, I defensively reacted to this suggestion like a mother who was watching her child being attacked and endangered. I told him that we could never let that happen. We had to fight to stay open and alive no matter what it cost us personally. Shutting down would be the worst thing that we could ever do, and given the theater's history, it could certainly never survive another closure. There would be no way we could ever come back from that. What we needed was support. And who was ever going to offer that to a theater that was boarded up and closed. Much as I respected and admired Stephen, I thought that was the most ridiculous and crazy idea I had ever heard. We had to find another way to deal with these challenges.

But even with that level of vehemence, a mind can be changed. A few months later I realized that he was right. There was no other way, and this was the mature, responsible and necessary way to go. He made his most persuasive though disconcerting case about this when he said to me one day, "This is the only way to find out if people care about the theater. The only way to find out if they care about *this* theater." That was an impossibly painful and dangerous reality to face, but face it we must as the long-term issues were not going away and the short-term challenges of staying alive from show to show with no guarantee that there would be a next one were becoming debilitating, exhausting and soul killing. Sadly, we did indeed have to go about carefully "shutting it down." We eventually referred to this in our surprising and painful announcements as taking a necessary intermission. That was a hopeful way of describing the process, but at that time, we had no real idea of whether there would be another act. There was hope, most certainly. But as we closed the doors, an act which garnered national publicity, the truth was that we had no certainty that we would ever be able to open them again.

I need not try to keep the suspense bubble up in the air. You know now that I spent not one but two decades at the theater, so this traumatic event was at the "ides of my tenure" and by far not the end of my run. In fact in some ways the best years were yet to come. So I will cut to the chase and say right now that we did get the doors open again, and the lights came back on and illuminated the building and the work on the stage. But there was a period of darkness before the resurrection when all of that was far from a sure thing.

The way in which that renaissance came about is actually a great story of luck, faith, inspiration, hard work and generosity. But before many of the good things happened, there were some very bleak days. Many times when the only person in the building was me and the only illumination in any of the dressing rooms, hallways, offices or onstage was the lone ghostlight on the stage which we left burning both by tradition and as a beacon of hope. The ghostlight and I developed a very special relationship.

Officially the building was shut down and off limits to anyone except a building inspector who would go in once a week to check for leaks, break-ins or infestation by our friendly theater rats. None of which occurred gratefully. But I was still in possession of my master key and my determination. So on several days and evenings I would sneak into the building, sit in the dark theater with my friend the ghostlight and literally will the theater back to life with a combination of prayer, a few tears and the not-infrequent transcendental conversations with Gilmor Brown, the theater's founder and resident ghost. I admit that my imagination is strong, but I swear that he came down the aisle one day and whispered in my ear, "Don't worry, it's going to be all right. Trust me." I told this story in the aftermath of our reopening, but not very much at the time that it took place for fear of being called madly optimistic. Or just insane. I feared being hauled off for treatment in a straightjacket. But honestly, those long hours alone in the darkness gave me an odd kind of comfort. At a certain point Gilmor and I both started to believe that the intermission would be temporary and that another act would follow this dark break. This was well before there was any realistic reason to believe that this was going to be true. Nevertheless, I would sit there and stare at the single bulb of the ghostlight and imagine a time when the stage and the house would once again be full of energy, artistry and vitally alive once again. I saw it clearly and without doubt. As the weeks went on and for many good reasons those moments started to occur more frequently and with even greater clarity. The ghostlight and I had many oddly wonderful hours together, somehow making sure that the theater stayed alive in the midst of the darkness, dreaming of a time when that single light would be joined by a hundred others and when I would have enthusiastic audiences in the rows beside me and my cherished fellow artists on the stage once again making the magic of the theater come alive.

And all of that happened! The how of how it happened is complicated and involved ... lawyers, judges, a supportive board of directors, and the good will of our audiences and supporters. Going through all of the legal machinations is a bit complicated and probably makes for better reading in a book on bankruptcy procedures than here. But there were some significant events that carry a definite theatrical flair that earn a place on these pages.

First of all, in answer to the question that Stephen Eich posed, we found out immediately that people did care. The closure of the theater brought about a huge outcry in the LA community and from all around the country. There were articles about this momentous event in newspapers, on television and radio and in many sources beyond the expected entertainment publications. Expressions of great concern and caring arrived from my colleagues all over the country, and they were both surprising and sustaining in their heartfelt sincerity. People cared about the theater, and yes, they cared about *this* theater. That became apparent very quickly.

However, I would be remiss if I did not come clean about the ugly and most painful side of this, made even uglier by the fact that it was borne of that old demon racism, which had been a factor that chased me throughout my time at the theater ever since my arrival. Remember me in the pot of boiling oil? It felt a bit like I was back in that fiery pot once again!

Not long after we shut the doors there were some very ugly, not very covert declarations that the closure had been brought about by my "Black agenda." There were repeated accusations from a surprising number of pundits that stated that this would never have happened if I had not been so intent on putting the work of artists of color on the stage with the intent to deliberately change the complexion of the audience. It was declared that the theater would not be in the sad shape that it was if the board of directors had been strong enough to stop the madness and prevent me from my personal crusade to "inflict" such radical diversity on an audience that clearly did not want that. According to these nasty voices, it was about time that I was run off, and not a moment too soon. And if it took shutting down the theater to accomplish that lynching, so be it. Yes, pretty ugly and frightening.

Not surprisingly, even though the facts were readily available and actually quite well known, there were truths that these naysayers (or idiots, depending on my mood) failed to point out as it would have obliterated their specious claims. They all failed to say that in addition to the work at the theater being balanced and extremely broad based in its appeal, they simply ignored the fact that the productions that had saved the theater many, many times were those that had appeal to our diverse audiences. *Play On!*, *Fences* and *Sister Act* among many others set box office records, and they filled our bank accounts at much-needed times. They also conveniently (or deliberately) failed to note that our efforts to achieve diversity on stage and off were being identified and rewarded with substantial grants from foundations and corporations supporting and encouraging our successes with hundreds of thousands of dollars for achieving something which would inspire the field, using The Playhouse as a shining beacon of hope in this area. No, this was rarely pointed out or acknowledged by those who wanted to insist that my "Black agenda" was the central problem which made it necessary to close. That charge, from a much larger number of ignoramuses than you would imagine, was as odious as those who felt during the Civil Rights Movement of the 1960s that integration would be the death of American society. Just as ignorant and equally repellant. But sadly, more than three decades later, there were those who felt strongly that it was the Black guy who had been the ruination of "their" precious theater, and it was about time for me to be run out of town and out of the building. I suddenly felt like the heat on that boiling pot of oil had been turned way up!

As you can imagine, this made a very painful and emotionally draining situation even more debilitating. This was not nearly the same as the physical pain of being held down in the streets, having the air pushed out of my lungs or, God forbid, the horrors of an actual lynching.

But the pain of this was deep. Very deep. Being confronted with this kind of outright racism combined with ignorance designed to smear me and eradicate all that I had done for the theater pushed me to some of the darkest days that I have had in my career. Dark, painful and emotionally lacerating. During this time, there were many, more in fact, who cared about my state and asked me how I was able to keep going. Here is something that White America should always remember. Black Americans are the descendants of slavery and the children of segregation. We have managed to stand up and press on not just through decades but through centuries of abuse and against unimaginable challenges. My father, when asked how he was doing, would answer until his 98th year on the earth, "I'm holdin' on." For years I always thought that this was just an idiosyncratic phrase of his own making. But I now believe that he was speaking both for himself and for those of color in this country who came before him, those that he grew up with and fought with. Ours is a culture of "holding on" and "moving on up a little higher," even in the face of the worst challenges, indignities, pain and suffering. My pain was deep and grievously distressing during this time. But I reminded myself that it was nothing like the deep and abiding struggles of those who had come before me, and that certainly helped to keep going. I was hurting, but I was not enslaved nor swinging from a tree. I felt "buked and scorned" indeed, but I had the strength of those who had come before me to lean on. I had strong shoulders on which to stand, and I was so grateful for that. As Black Americans we all have that, thank God. At the worst of times, I listened to the words of my father and I kept holding on.

With that tenacity of my ancestors and with those words ringing in my ears, I held on and I pressed on, as I always had and as I always would. But I confess that there were many moments when these outrageous and totally inaccurate slanders on top of everything else that I was dealing with tempted me to throw in the towel. Or tie a very heavy rock around it and sling it back towards the mudslingers who wrote and said such things. Of course, that would only prove to them that I was just another angry Black man, as they always suspected, adding fuel to their already racist fire. So, I never addressed that issue; I just pressed on to prove them wrong. To be honest, I think those smears actually fueled my own fire and made me even more determined to get the theater reopened, not only because I passionately wanted that to be true but also to shove some crow down the throats of those who vocally attacked me in this way. I could not think of any better way to shut them up than to accomplish the miracle of rebirth. I remembered those valuable words from Lloyd Richards many years earlier and kept my eyes on the prize. Getting the doors open and those lights blazing brightly once again was a truly valuable prize to pursue and far more important than spending time and energy defending myself against the false charges of haters and racist mudslingers.

Several incredibly valuable and incredibly lucky factors soon came into play which made attaining that prize in what turned out to be a shockingly short amount of time possible. First and foremost was the kind offer by a powerful and highly respected law firm to take on our bankruptcy case on a pro bono basis. Lord knows we would never have been able to afford them or the process in any other way. They simply believed that it was important for the theater to be saved and continue the good work that we were doing both for our community and the broader field. They very quickly jumped into the deep end of the pool and advised us on what legal route to take. Their incredibly good advice kept us from obliterating the existing not-for-profit organization and both our structural and physical assets. That was a very smart and wise legal maneuver that saved huge amounts of time and money and kept the existing producing company alive.

Second, and equally important, was the goodwill of our existing audience and supporters. With their donations, yes, of course. But during this process they had a vitally important choice to make that would allow us to move forward or force us to collapse. In the legal process that the company followed under the guidance of our smart and benevolent legal team, we were able to get rid of most of our existing debts, most particularly the age-old bank loans which frankly had been paid many times over in exorbitant interest rates. The obligation that remained in place was to our subscribers. When we were forced to close, at the beginning of the season, they were still owed five of six productions that they had paid for and we had collected the money. We were obligated to offer them a choice of how this obligation would be satisfied. They could either donate that sum back to the theater, be patient and wait to be given the remaining five productions, or they could ask for a refund. That final choice could have spelled disaster if in fact people really did not care and wanted their money back. A quick and strictly legal response came back from the thousands of subscribers who were offered this choice. That response was lifesaving. Of those thousands, many took the first choice, most opted for the second ("I don't want the money back; I just want to see the shows!") and fewer than 100 actually asked for a refund. That loyalty from our existing audience literally allowed us to press forward, keeping our eyes on the prize!

Of course, this was far from the last of our challenges. Though a fair but honestly supportive judge was able to do a great deal to help us through the process, he was still obligated to require us to prove that we had funding in place to continue operations and to have the ability to move ahead as a "going concern." Put simply, this meant that we needed not only goodwill but the bucks to get back to work, pay for the productions we owed, support a staff and pay the utilities bill to keep those lights shining once they were back on. This proved to be our greatest challenge. But remember that God that sometimes is there so quickly? Sitting in the dark communing with Gilmor and that ghostlight, I may have also said a prayer or two. Or ten or a hundred! And that heavenly arrival was not long in coming.

Very shortly after the doors closed, I was asked to do an interview with Patt Morrison, a very popular *LA Times* columnist. A tough but fair and honest writer. She wanted to know how I was feeling and how I was holding up. I put on my most optimistic and hopeful face, of course. Because I staunchly referred to this as an intermission, not a closure, intended to put things in order and then to get back in business, she asked me what it would take financially to get the theater up and running again. I confess now, as this was early in the process, that I actually did not have a concrete answer. But never one to be thrown off by silly statistics when the life of art is in the offing, I came up with a figure and told her that $2,000,000 would most certainly allow us to get the doors open and allow us to produce one more. Given what next occurred, I've often thought in hindsight that perhaps I should have said five! But in the moment, that amount seemed doable, not scary, and in fact turned out to be pretty exact. And, again in hindsight, which is not always 20/20, the larger amount might have actually dampened the good fortune which soon blessedly came our way.

That interview came out in the Sunday edition of the paper. As I recall on the editorial pages, not in the entertainment section. Thank goodness that there are some arts supporters who read every section! Just a couple of days later, I got a call as I sat in our now empty offices. I recognized both the name and the voice of the caller, so I knew that all was legit. I might well have been skeptical otherwise. He asked me quite calmly if the $2,000,000 number that I had quoted in the interview was correct. I stood my ground and confidently answered affirmatively, expecting perhaps an argument or a discussion, but not his next response. He told me that he and his wife were prepared to provide us with half of that amount, with a gift of $1,000,000. My inner heavenly voices began to sing immediately, I suspect. I quieted them long enough to hear him say that there were three conditions: The gift was to be made anonymously. The gift had to be matched to bring the total to the posited $2,000,000. And finally, as the gift was in support of the theater but also specifically in support of me, I had to promise that when and if the theater reopened that I would not run off to any greener pastures right away. I am not sure how he knew it, or even if he knew it, but in fact during this time I was being wooed by a couple of other theaters and by some commercial theater opportunities in New York City. It was also true that prior to this crisis I had made a noise or two about possibly moving on after more than a full decade at the theater; I just had not announced that publicly. But once again, he seemed to know or at least suspect that this might be true. As a result, condition number three.

I took a big breath, made a quick personal choice, swallowed heavily and told him that we would honor all of those requests, including the one that pertained to me and my near future. I knew very quickly that making that promise was what I had to do. But also what I wanted to do. I wanted to do whatever it took to keep the theater alive!

"Done!" he said, "Let us know when you get the other money together, and we will write the check." The heavenly voices started to sing more loudly, even though at that moment I had no idea where the matching funds would come from. But, without a whole bunch of legal documents and a bit of wrangling over some details, the deal was as sealed as it could be in that ten-minute conversation. A ten-minute conversation which made me feel pretty secure at that moment that I would not be sitting alone in the dark forever.

But there was still much work to be done before that could happen. When I informed those fancy lawyers about this lightning bolt of luck, they were, as lawyers often are, quite skeptical and would remain so until that wrangling and paperwork got done. But they did feel that the number that I had wildly positioned would be persuasive to the judge ... IF we could raise the matching million and prove to said judge that we truly had a majority of that amount in an escrow account or at least signed and secure pledges from other donors. Stephen Eich was also quite skeptical. As I did not initially reveal the name of the $1,000,000 donor to him, I think that he believed that I was being delusional or that this call had never happened. It took my revealing their identity and the source of their fortune and a subsequent meeting with them to convince him that in fact I was not hallucinating. But he quickly moved on to skepticism that we would be able to raise the matching funds, or at least that we could raise them quickly.

He was not wrong to have question marks about that, I confess. Raising $1,000,000 for an arts institution that was closed was not a small challenge. But I blithely ignored that reality.

I have to give credit to the theater's board for helping me to take on the challenge. Once they actually believed that the $1,000,000 gauntlet that had been thrown down was legitimate, they did rise to the occasion and managed to commit to raising half of the needed matching dollars, most of it coming from their own resources. While always supportive, at least as individuals they were not as a whole a fundraising board. So beyond making their collective pledges I knew that they could not be relied on to complete the challenge.

Another "so quickly" moment amazingly arrived at just the right time. I got another one of those propitious calls shortly after that *LA Times* article came out. This one from an associate of a NYC producer who I soon learned had studied at The Playhouse School of Drama many years before. She wanted to come by and see the theater, even in its woefully darkened state, and to talk with me about what she might do to help. I met her on one of our few cold and windy Southern California days, using that lucky master key of mine to get us into the building. As I opened the alley door that led into the lobby, a gust of wind rushed past us and into the building, stirring up a small tornado of dust and leaves that had built up as the janitors were not servicing the building regularly. They could be seen only dimly in the shaft of light that burst into the theater from the side door that I opened, a sad but very theatrical effect. One that immediately made me feel quite melancholy as it reminded me in a visceral way that this could be the state of the theater for a while if things didn't go well. I turned to look at her, and I could tell that she was equally sad to see our beautiful lobby in this condition. The sadness in her eyes matched that in mine. She quickly recovered and said, "Something's got to be done about this," and it was clear that she did not just mean the leaves and the dust. I did not argue with her. But I did tuck that clearly heartfelt and determined declaration into the ever-plotting memory bank of my brain. Weeks later when we faced that critical juncture of completing the $1,000,000 match, I remembered that moving moment. During the intervening time, I learned that she was a woman of considerable resources, though I certainly did not know how considerable. But I guessed, or hopefully imagined, that they were abundant enough that she might be able to help in this situation and/or that she might be willing to reach out to a couple of her producing partners who could help push us closer to our goal. Without knowing how much if anything I could reasonably expect to come out of it, I called her. Future fundraisers remember, never be afraid to call. There are no other steps until you take that first one. I updated her on the current situation, the need to raise $2,000,000, the proffered $1,000,000 gift that needed a match, the $500,000 in pledges that had come from board members and a few other sources (including me) and the need to raise another equal amount. I laid all of this out and ended my précis of the situation by saying meekly, "I'm wondering if you can help me with this or if you might be willing to speak with anyone that you think might be helpful." As I did not know her very well at that point, I felt the most pregnant of pauses and my hopes slipping down the hill and out the door. Just as I took a breath to say, "Of course, I'm not expecting you to solve the rest of the challenge," she spoke up, and I shut up! And wisely so. "Well," she said, "Yes, I can do that. I can give you the other $500,000." The breath that I was holding that I blessedly had not released to intone those alternative off-the-hook-letting words now exclaimed something truly lofty and eloquent, "Really?" Something profound like that, as I remember. It can actually be difficult to be lofty and eloquent when a completely unexpected moment parts the clouds and allows the glorious rays of the sun to shine through. Really!

That joyous moment was followed by yet more skepticism, a good deal of legal wrangling, some initial concerns followed by certainties and celebration, and finally this piece of the puzzle was firmly in place. The initial gift had been matched, and we were now able to go to the judge with all things in place to move into the final phases of the process. Then, if all went as planned and as hoped for, we would have our fiscal freedom and the ability to open once again. It would be a cautious, careful and initially small-scaled reopening. But one that would allow the theater to be inhabited again by more than just the spirit of Gilmor, the ghostlight and me.

For legal reasons, we had to keep the large gifts and the quick process confidential for a fairly long period of time. So in the public eye it did not seem that we were doing very much or moving forward in any focused way. As a result the odious racial charges intensified and were amplified by accusations from those same naysayers and others that we were not doing anything to solve the problems and get the theater reopened. My triple Scorpio nature makes me very good at keeping secrets, but I confess that holding my tongue and not responding to these continued charges and accusations needed a Herculean effort of restraint. But once again, I pressed on with my head held high and my mouth tightly shut. But like a cat with the canary, I had a very good secret, and for the very best of reasons I was able to bite my eager-to-reply tongue!

ACT VII, SCENE ONE

Coming Out of the Dark

I think that I've kept you in the dark with me and the ghostlight for long enough. It is time to give you the 4-1-1 on the miraculous $1,000,000 donors who saved the day. Even in this revelation there is a bit of a hidden surprise.

Many of you will know the name Mike Stoller. Many more of you will recognize this name as one half of the hugely successful songwriting team Leiber and Stoller. And I suspect that all of the rest of you will know the titles and perhaps even the words and the music of some of their greatest hits including "Hound Dog," "Stand by Me," "Yakety Yak," "Spanish Harlem," and Peggy Lee's late career success "Is That All There Is?" among many, many others. Their huge song catalogue was celebrated in the successful Broadway revue *Smokey Joe's Cafe*. It was Mike Stoller who called me on that auspicious day with the offer of the generous $1,000,000 gift. I, of course, made the assumption that royalties and publishing income over many years made such largesse possible, and that is certainly true in part. However, I was soon to learn that Mike's wife, Corky Hale Stoller, one of the few women instrumentalists of her era that came to her own fame for playing harp—often jazz harp—was the one who really pushed for making this gift. In addition to the resources from their music careers, it turns out that Corky's mother had founded a huge department store chain in the Midwest and that her large fortune had recently made its way into the hands of Corky and her siblings. This gave Corky the freedom to be a very generous donor to a number of social and political causes. (She kept a life-sized photo statue of Barack Obama outside of her front door for months after he had been elected.) She was an avid reader of the *LA Times* editorial pages, and she generously and quickly responded to that fateful article and encouraged Mike to help her save the day. We might have been able to come out of that intermission in other ways. But there is no doubt that this was a true lifesaving miracle that moved that process along and allowed us to

---

151

come out of the dark much more quickly than we anticipated. We honored Corky and Mike a couple of years later at a gala on the opening night of The Playhouse production of *Smokey Joe's Cafe*. I privately honored and appreciated them both on many, many other days. The ghostlight and I said at least one prayer of thanks as we sat in the dark of the theater together. They were truly our theatrical heroes!

All of this good fortune and the incredible efforts of our legal team and a supportive case judge allowed us to move through the bankruptcy process with nearly unheard of speed. What had been predicted to take at least one year and perhaps as long as two or three was actually accomplished in about nine months! I am grateful to all of the heroes who got us through that dark period and into the light so quickly. The lawyers, the judge, our donors and supporters, and especially the colleagues and artists who helped me to keep the faith and carry on. I did it with them, and I did it for them. I wanted us all to walk into the light of the theater once again and simply get back to doing what we do. When a *NY Times* reporter who was doing a story about reopening the theater asked me, "What happens next?" my answer was a pretty simple one, "Now we get back to work."

That is exactly what we did. The doors of the theater closed in February; we took a longer than usual intermission and came back with a show in October. The well-known actor Ed Asner helped us to get the lights burning again with his much-acclaimed one-man show based on FDR. We followed that with a production of a show called *Uptown/Downtown*, which illustrated the remarkable career of my good friend Leslie Uggams. Yes, that same Leslie that I had adored from my balcony seat so many, many years ago, who also toured to great success in my production of *Blue* many years later. Shortly after we got back to "full scale" productions with a new musical called *Twist*, an adaptation of the Dickens' story that was directed and choreographed by Debbie Allen. There was no question about the energy of the theater returning when that show burst onto the stage.

I was overjoyed to move through this dark and trying period so quickly. But as all of the pieces big and small began to fall into place and it started to become clear that we were going to be able to reopen, I confess that I did have another fear. I was afraid that we would come back as a lesser organization than we had been, reduced in ambition, smaller in scale, and I dreaded most the thought that we would be open, but only open and not the shining palace of art that we had been for my first decade at the theater. That kind of return would have been even more painful than all the rest. For everyone, I think, but certainly for me, as I had made "that deal" to stay at the theater if the miracle of renaissance was accomplished. I had pushed hard, worked long hours and drained my sweat glands to fulfill the vision of building a great theater over my first decade. I truly dreaded the thought of leading a lesser organization that was just limping through and not really dreaming bigger dreams. We all had to accept that reality for a while (though small does not have to mean not worthy of attention, as the intimate shows with Ed Asner and Leslie Uggams ably demonstrated).

With a few more prayers, a bit more sweat and determination, and a lot more hard work, I can gratefully say that it wasn't very long until we were completely "back" and functioning just as we had been before that long intermission. In many ways the miracle that was even bigger than getting the place open again was that some of the best years were ahead of and not behind me. Not only did we get the lights shining again, but often shining even more brightly than they had before. In our marketing for the season after we reopened, I pushed for us to use the lyrics from a well-known Cy Coleman and Dorothy Fields song, "The Best Is Yet to Come." A very good title, a very good and clever lyric, but gratefully, an even better reality! Many on the marketing staff felt that I was being hyperbolic and perhaps even tempting fate. But in fact some of the best was yet to come during my ten-year-long second act at Pasadena Playhouse.

Act VII, Scene Two

Making an Exit (A Long One!)

While it certainly is true that some great years and wonderful seasons of theater followed the Dark Period of the Intermission, I confess that it is also true that somewhere deep in my soul, once I knew that the theater was back in "fighting shape" and producing again at its previous level of quality, success and energy, I started to make plans to gracefully and happily "Exit Stage Right." Hopefully not pursued by a bear!

There were many reasons for this. First of all, it was my very strong belief that my generation of artistic leaders should not repeat what I regarded and many agreed was the mistake of many of the founding fathers and mothers of regional theaters. From my point of view many of them were guilty of "staying too long at the fair," with tenures lasting over 30 years. In many of those cases it was pretty well known that feet were being tapped and whispered conversations were taking place in the hallways and corridors of the theater about just when so and so was going to leave. Sometimes those deliberately loud stage whispers were intended to be overheard. Or there were really ugly private scenes that inevitably became public, involving boards and theater staffs practically pushing some of those much-to-be-respected but desperately clinging-on legends out of the door, sometimes with a real lack of graciousness. I certainly did not want that to be the case for me. My point of view was that it would be good for the theater and good for me to make that graceful exit at a point when everyone still wanted me to stay! That was far preferable from my point of view and so much better for the theater. On the simplest level, I believed and still believe that the life of a theater (or perhaps any performing arts organization) needs to be refreshed at some point by a change of leadership.

I felt that after what would soon be 20 years under my artistic leadership that the time had come to hit that refresh button, both for the sake of the theater and for my own health, sanity and artistic growth.

I honestly did not think that it would be quite so LONG an exit.

I had always committed myself both emotionally and contractually to five-year sojourns at this artistic home. We emerged from the intermission a couple of years before my 15th anniversary as the theater's artistic leader. It seems that every time I took a breath to announce that I would be leaving something occurred to "pull me back in." In this case it was often good things, including substantial grants for new initiatives that I wanted to pursue. Or it might be that an executive or managing director beat me to the punch and announced that they were leaving just as that breath to speak was filling my own lungs. As they got the jump on me and announced their intentions before I did, it seemed best to stay. To avoid an endless repetition of that rondelet, I took a breath faster and spoke more quickly this time, two years before my 20th anniversary, and announced my absolute intention to take my leave. I got it out strongly at that point for all of the reasons that I've described above. Also because of some less-than-wonderful things were in the air at the company which made my departure a stronger necessity for me. But before we get to that.... Here are a few more high points when we were riding the crest of the wave that filled my second decade at the theater.

Art/The Heiress/Fallen Angels and *A Song at Twilight*

There was a feeling among some that perhaps it would be difficult to attract the same level of artists to the theater following the intermission or that the quality of the productions would be diminished. The latter was just as worrisome to me as the intermission itself. I had many a nightmare about the theater reopening as less than what it had been. So I am very proud of the fact that these four superlative revivals of American and British classics included such wonderful actors as Bradley Whitford, Richard Chamberlain, Sharon Lawrence and Bruce Davidson along with many others in productions that were rich, vital, beautifully designed and directed and worthy of the attention that had to be paid to their high quality and the freshness that was brought to what might be considered old chestnuts. Not so in this case. These productions felt immediate, alive with life and amazingly necessary for the moment when they were on our stage thanks to splendid directors like David Lee, Art Manke and my extremely gifted Associate Artistic

The zany and wonderful company of *Art*: (left to right) Bradley Whitford, Michael O'Keffe, and Roger Bart, in 2012 (photograph by Jim Cox).

Director Dámaso Rodriguez (who I am proud to say went on to become an artistic director at a theater all his own—another accomplishment that gave me great pride).

There is something that I still ponder about this grouping of plays and several others that I chose to include in the seasons over the years. At the time I was only conscious of loving these plays and feeling that they deserved reconsideration because of the quality of the writing and the vivid stories that they told. But in retrospect, I wonder. I wonder if, on some subconscious level, I made choices about many of these plays in response to those who in my early days expected that I was going to "blackenize" the theater. Or was it a retroactive response in some way to those vicious tongues which wagged about my Black agenda during the theater's short closure. Was there somewhere in my thinking a hidden desire to prove that I could successfully produce "my stuff and their stuff" with equal skill and theatrical vibrance? I want to tell myself no, that this was not the case. These were just plays that I greatly respected and that needed to be seen once again. But was it in fact that "White gaze" that pushed me in this direction? Was the little White man sitting on my shoulder once again? Or were the little White men and women whispering in my ear, "Bet you can't do it 'our' way?" Was I still feeling a need to prove something, even after a decade of proving some-things? I hope not! But I wonder if that was at play at all or on any level. In some ways it does not matter because this was programming to be proud of and productions that were rightly celebrated. That matters more than anything else. And beyond that, I was also proud of this—the many things that I did without worrying about that odious White gaze, either ignoring or simply not caring about the whispers in my ear. Even needing to wonder, then and now is the burden of being chased by race that artists of color are always forced to bare. But we press on. And once again, I did.

Blues for an Alabama Sky/Intimate Apparel/ Twelve Angry Men

You will not hear me say (or write) this often, but during my home stretch at the theater I directed three really exquisite productions of two plays written by brilliant Black playwrights and revival of an American classic in a new concept that brought racial issues to the forefront at a much-needed time and made an old play feel brand new. They were all highlights of my second decade at The Playhouse.

Once again, I had a great encounter with the *Blues*, this time as part of the title of Pearl Cleage's brilliant and evocative tribute to the Harlem Renaissance period, *Blues for an Alabama Sky*, which depicts the sad, funny, tragic and ultimately triumphant story of the play's heroine, Angel. In my mind this role is every bit as challenging and as rewarding for both actresses and audiences as the part of Blanche DuBois in *A Streetcar Named Desire*, another lady of the night with a mysterious background who also depends on the kindness of strangers, just as Angel does. In my production the role was played with ferocity, fierce energy and sensuality by Robin Givens, who, I believe, surprised everyone with her incredible strength and range on the stage. Though Robin had enjoyed a very long and successful television career and was well known for a less-than-satisfying relationship with the great fighter (unfortunately in more ways than one) Mike Tyson. The details of that "romance" had perhaps put Robin under the radar for a while before we went into production for the play. But I could sense when we first met to talk about her doing the production that she was ready. Ready to work, ready for a challenge, and ready to have a triumph that would remind people that whatever else they thought, she was an Actress with a capital A! For everyone who saw her wonderful performance in this play there was no doubt that she is. The company also included Kevin Carroll and Kadeem Hardison, both of whom were well known from their work on stage and television, and a less-well-known but wonderfully talented young woman named Tessa Thompson. Tessa had established a strong reputation in local theater productions by this time, and shortly following her lovely work in this play she would explode on the screen and become a true movie star. I am so proud of her. It was a wonderful, giving, and deeply talented company of actors who truly made Harlem come alive in this beautiful, funny and very moving play.

I don't think that there is a better playwright in America right now, of any color or any gender, than Lynn Nottage. She is quite simply a great American playwright on the same level as Tennessee Williams, August Wilson, Lillian Hellman and Tony Kushner, and she is now at long last getting all of the attention and acclaim that is so well deserved. Not to mention two Pulitzer Prizes, among many other rewards. For me what is so surprising about Lynn is her phenomenal range. She seems

Lovely Robin Givens in my production of *Blues for an Alabama Sky*, 2011 (photograph by Jim Cox).

to be able to write with equal brilliance in almost any style from gut-wrenching drama to high-style comedy to contemporary plays which clearly and resolutely reflect social and political concerns of our country right now. I had the joy of directing Lynn's beautiful, lyrical and romantic play *Intimate Apparel*, which celebrates America's diversity in another era but with an emotional edge that makes it feel so very much of the moment. It examines relationships between people of all colors, religions and varying social backgrounds and their desire to connect against sometimes impossible odds. The play is filled with music and language that is almost like poetry and every bit as hypnotic and dazzling. Lynn's beautiful and often wrenching dialogue combined with equally haunting and beautiful music that I chose from the lesser-known works of Scott Joplin were simply transporting. Another won-derful cast and a great design team evoked the period and told this lovely story in a way that produced true theatrical magic and which gave me one of my most reward-ing experiences and yet another great success for the theater.

A great bonus was that the diversity that I so hoped for in the audience was reflected onstage as well in the interweaving of these characters from disparate worlds and dif-ferent social classes all coming together in their desperate searches for love and connection. By this time the rainbow of colors on the stage was also seated in the theater. I was proud of the pro-duction but perhaps even

My wonderfully diverse and beautiful com-pany of *Intimate Apparel*, 2012. Left to right, back row David St. Louis, Kristy Johnson, Angel Reda, and Adam Smith; front row Vanessa E. Williams and Dawnn Lewis.

more proud of achieving that goal. Not for the first or only time did we get it right—both onstage and off.

This commitment to frequent and absolute diversity throughout our theater became a beacon of our theatrical life at Pasadena Playhouse. This mixture of Black and White, along with works which appealed to the Latino community such as *Anna in the Tropics* and *Real Women Have Curves* and productions such as a new musical called *Waterfall* based on a hugely popular Thai romance novel which delivered Asian Americans to our theater, all made for a sublimely diverse audience which was celebrated in the national community and even envied by them. When asked how we achieved this by fellow theater leaders I would often respond somewhat glibly but also truthfully, "Fire yourself and hire a person of color in a leadership position at your theater." There were many things which made it happen. Most notably a constant diet of diversity in the programming and sincere outreach efforts to these communities. But I do believe that part of the reason for our notable achievement in this area is that people of color came out to our theater and came over and over again because they were there to support me as much as the specific play or the overall work of the theater. They were eager for "one of their own," a person of color to be successful in leading a theatrical company of this size. Finally the American Theatre as a whole seems to be getting that message! I am thrilled to celebrate the announcements of BIPOC leaders at major theaters all over our country in far greater numbers over the past several years. Let us hope that this good trend continues.

However, the cries of racial strife were far from over. As much as we were beginning to overcome both at my theater and in our country, there were clearly times during those years (and there are clearly times now) when our racial divides are glaringly prominent, disappointing, heartbreaking and even dangerous. One of those moments in time prompted my production of *Twelve Angry Men* using a very specific conceptual approach that was entirely "in the moment."

This came about shortly after the decision in the Trayvon Martin case, when those who were guilty of his murder somehow through the power of white privilege had the charges against them dismissed. This caused racial violence and uprisings all over the country, a series of events that would be repeated and all too sadly necessary in the years ahead. In response to both the verdict and the violence, President Obama made the first speech in which he confronted his own very personal feelings about this case and more widely about the issues of race in America directly and in a dynamically moving way. He spoke bravely and emotionally about his knowledge that Trayvon could have been a child of his and that he could well be the parent of a young Black boy facing a legal system which simply ignored the facts and rushed to judgments that did not represent justice in any way.

I was moved as I always was by the eloquence and brilliance of President Obama's words and in this case by his clear display of emotion. Something that many of our presidents are not brave enough to allow. In this case, I was more vitally moved to action and not just tears! I determined that the theater MUST put something on the stage that dealt with the issues that were swirling around us like a plague at that moment. Sadly, that would continue for many years ahead and actually be quite literally an extension of a plague in our nation in a few years to come. I thought it was vital to put something on our stage which thrust our audiences into confronting the fact that the racial divide in our country was as strong as ever.

Facing that strongly and truly acknowledging that reality would force us all into a conversation about race that would push us forward. Acknowledgment after all is the first step towards cure. There would be no curing the problem without admitting that the problem exists.

My good friend "theatrical instinct" pushed me to go back and read Reginald Rose's well-known *play Twelve Angry Men,* which I knew well from the Sidney Lumet film and from seeing it onstage several times. Something told me that there might be something mined there that would "hold the mirror up to mankind" in a way that could be powerful at that very moment. With a fresh reading of the play, an idea began to form in my mind of doing the play with a cast that was equally divided between six Black characters and six White. Without changing the dialogue, except for a few small references, it was clear right away that a profound subtext would emerge for the play's original dialogue that would, somewhat sadly, be immediate and current. This was especially true in terms of the play's condemnation of the justice system when dealing with a young person of color. In that very moment there was also great resonance regarding the way that we still bring biases, prejudices and preconceptions into the room with us, and even more important, come to decisions and unity at different times and in different ways. But we can actually "get there" if indeed we actually are willing to listen or if we are in a situation where we are forced to listen. Perhaps the latter can be preferable in some ways. Maybe we can only truly listen when we are in situations where we are "trapped" and will only be released from bondage when we let go of our prejudices and walk into the light of genuine truth ... as in a jury room. (One hopes!)

This casting concept for the play proved to provide the fuel to ignite valuable and important conversations. These deeply moving dialogues took place during our rehearsal process, in performance, and in debates in the lobby after the curtain came down.

We had a fascinating rehearsal process which involved sitting around the table that would eventually be a part of our set itself, honestly discussing race not so much as a political issue but as a personal one. The actors slowly but surely started to reveal instances in their lives when they had been victims of racial prejudice, where they had witnessed it and done nothing, and—perhaps most bravely—when they had actually operated from a place of privilege and used their own racial power either consciously or unconsciously. Those conversations were brave, painful, occasionally humorous, angry, sometimes shocking and hugely helpful. They infused into the production a level of reality and inner life that made the decades-old play seem just birthed. And they helped to establish a level of trust within the company that allowed the racial animosity within the context of the play to be revealed in a way that was vicious, ugly and fully realized. Given that, the journey to justice in the case being tried in this room was emotionally fraught and theatrically electric. The play had both its inherent power and a kind of electricity that perhaps it had never had before. In a way, it was America and its lack of REAL racial equality that was on trial here. That was what was being debated and worked through. The ability of these men to fight their way through it to a unanimous verdict offered up something that we needed at that very moment and that we still need—hope.

The production was hailed on the theatrical level but also for pushing our audiences into thoughts, reflections and conversations about race. There were, of course, those who felt that this was part of ye old Black agenda of mine and that I had desecrated an American classic. Shockingly, some even said that doing the play with this concept was disingenuous and unnecessary because there was no racial problem in American anymore. Sadly, I kid you not. That was actually stated at a post-show discussion by a young white man who stated that he knew "Because he went to Yale"! Once more, I kid you not, that is a quote. I believe that I had to be restrained by one of the actors as I started to

A tense moment with my *12 Angry Men*, featuring Jason George, Gregory North and the full company in 2013 (photograph by Jim Cox).

leap off the stage and chase this deluded Yalie up the aisle and out of the theater. I wonder if he was still professing that offensive theory several years later? Is it possible that he continued to be a "race denier" as George Floyd was lying on the street as a police officer pushed the breath out of his body with his knee on his neck? Was he still saying that the problems were over when America reacted to this and far-too-many other violent acts towards men and women of color with looting, rioting in the streets and repeated cries of how much "Black Lives Matter"? I suspect, in fact I know, that it sadly is possible. Very sadly.

At the time that we first mounted the play I remember telling the acting company that I hoped that this concept highlighting the increased racial divide in our country would not be relevant or necessary in the future. Again, quite sadly, the administration of the president of our country who followed President Obama greatly exacerbated rather than soothed racial tensions. During the years of his tenure, our nation was more divided than ever. When I was asked to remount the play using the same concept a few years later at Ford's Theatre in Washington, DC, I took on the assignment with necessity but a bit of a broken heart given that igniting those discussions and facing the reality of racial discrimination was still a burning issue in our country. If anything, the play felt even more immediate and relevant in that production, and the discussions that followed those performances were just as fiery and impassioned. It is worthy to note that this time the production took place in the theater where Lincoln was assassinated, and the resulting dialogues happened just a few blocks from the White House. I wondered if the current occupant was aware or listening to what was being said on this important topic. I somehow doubt it. But others were moved, angered, impassioned and motivated by our work, and that is to be celebrated.

A Night with Janis Joplin

Over my many years at the theater I would frequently walk through the beautiful courtyard of The Playhouse into the lobby and wind up at the top of the house left aisle of the theater. This was often during the course of a performance when I would drift in at various points to check on a show during its run. Just before I would open the doors between the lobby and the house I would often have a moment of trepidation about whether the back rows of the theater would be full or not. Well, not every time, as there were many productions that were, knock on wood, sold out on a consistent basis. I was always more than happy not to be able to find a seat in the back rows or on the far aisle. It gave me great joy when I had to lean against the wall because there were no seats to be had. That was the case for every performance of a beautiful celebration of the great rock singer Janis Joplin, which was created by my friend and respected colleague Randy Johnson.

We first produced this show in 2013, about two and a half years after the "intermission." (We would actually bring it back for another run during the summer of the following year.) The production rocked, due to the leading character and the leading lady, Mary Bridget Davies who embodied Janis in an uncanny and brilliant way. The lady's music, Mary's remarkable voice, a slammin' band and the Black female singers who supported our lead created a kind of energy in the theater that literally shook the wall against which I was leaning. I think that I loved this particular vantage point because it offered a clear view of the stage but also of the audience. In this case it was a thrill to watch both, which I did frequently.

The show was another great success for the theater, once again setting box office records. But for me it represented a kind of personal success that had nothing to do with ticket sales and house counts. Many months after the run at Pasadena, the show would be produced on Broadway, garnering a Tony nomination for Mary. Whatever might be said about the show, it had an undeniable energy that was the result of the performances, the evocation of Janis's spirit and the incredible music that seemed to be a kind of "youth elixir" for the audience. It was not uncommon to see theater patrons who were well into their 60s (or older) jumping out of their seats and dancing in the aisles, suddenly finding a renewed strength, energy and vigor that they had perhaps not displayed in many years. They were transported back to Woodstock, to rock concerts and to basements with blaring stereos by the experience. There were few times during my entire tenure at the theater that I felt that the room was more ALIVE than during these performances. There was a palpable energy coming from off the stage, out into the house and then given back to the performers by the audience. A circle of energy that gave the building a theatrical pulse which made the theater seem to vibrate and shiver with excitement. For me, this was a great personal reward. As one who had sat there in the dark for so many weeks, alone with the ghostlight, it was thrilling to see the theater so fully brimming with undeniable life! Whatever moments of fear I had during that dark time, and there were many such moments, this was what I envisioned and prayed for. A theater that was once again "on fire," as my father would say. On fire with theatricality, blazing performances, and incendiary reactions from our patrons. It was what I hoped, dreamed and prayed for while sitting there alone in the dark. And now it was a reality as I leaned against the wall and observed the theatrical fire burning once again. Magic....

Kiss Me Kate

I felt that magic once again a couple of seasons later when I mounted a dream project of mine. A production of Cole Porter's classic musical *Kiss Me Kate*, with a group of supremely gifted African American actor/singers in the leading roles, including Wayne Brady and Merle Dandridge who led the company supremely with dazzling and soulful performances. I guess you could call it "Black Magic" in this case. And deservedly so! This production brought together many of the things that I had always loved in the theater. The great works of Shakespeare, the joys of musical comedy, and in this version, the incredible brilliance and joy of Black musical theater performers that I had discovered so many years ago when I was sitting in the second balcony of all of those Broadway theaters. It was a great pleasure to have the chance to pour into this production my great affection for all of these aspects of my life in the theater.

I must say that I have never been one for what I have often called "dipped in chocolate" versions of plays or musicals. I use that term about productions where there is a well-intended but arbitrary decision made to cast Black actors without any strong concept or point of view in mind. I disagree with that very strongly. But when the choice is well considered, the material examined and the concept thought through thoroughly, I believe that the use of what I call "color conscious" casting can yield very rich rewards. As opposed to those instances where "color-blind" casting is the order of the day. I personally find that a pretty odious term and think that it is fairly ridiculous as we do not live in a color-blind society. There is no way for you to have people leave their racial perceptions at the door. I've often said that people who believe in color-blind casting should not be allowed to drive! That is not the way to achieve diversity in existing material. But carefully considered, the use of actors of color in roles previously played primarily by white actors can yield not just more employment opportunities but new and rich rewards from even the most well-known material.

I felt that my idea was a sound one in this case. I wanted to do this production as a kind of homage to the great African American touring companies that existed in the first half of the last century. I hoped that it would also be a celebration of those brave but lesser-known Black classical actors such as Ira Aldredge and Canada Lee and a tribute to the much more famous and frequently controversial icon Paul Robeson as well. Many years of researching Black theatrical history in America had made me aware that there was something of a tradition going back many years of taking existing classical material and adapting it to the talents of Black performers. This resulted in such productions as the *Hot Mikado*, which starred Bill Bojangles Robinson, and even more apt to this situation, a musical adaptation of Shakespeare's *A Midsummer Night's Dream* called *Swingin' the Dream*, which starred the great Louis Armstrong as the mischievous character Puck.

In Cole Porter's musical, people often forget that the acting company is not actually doing Shakespeare's play; they are performing a musical version of *The Taming of the Shrew*. So the idea of doing the show with a Black acting company actually fit like a glove and gave literal new color and meaning to the text and wonderful jazz, gospel and bluesy inflections to many of Porter's songs (although the show-within-the-show material was delivered exactly as originally conceived and written).

Without changing a word—well, maybe we changed one or two words—we deservedly honored Black performers in a lesser-known chapter of theater history and also brought new verve and theatrical pizazz to an American musical theater classic. The success of the concept was most dynamically on display in the opening of the second act when this dazzling cast turned up the heat even higher on the song "Too Darn Hot." With the addition of dance arrangements that hinted at Africanic rhythms and fiery licks from the horn section, it was hot indeed! The second act opened, and the show was stopped immediately at the end of that number.

The production was widely praised. The *LA Times* critic called it "An ingenious adaptation" and noted the "thrilling bluesy sound" of the score. Theatremania wrote, "Pasadena Playhouse infuses Cole Porter's classic with a taste of jazz and soul. The production has many dazzling moments." And the wonderful cheerleader Steven Stanley wrote in *Stage SceneLA*, "A much needed tribute to little known African-American trailblazers.... A 'Kiss Me Kate' unlike any you've seen before. Thrillingly reinvigorated." Clearly these smart critics and others got it!

The acting company for this production bonded immediately in an exceptional and palpable way that was tangible and gave an ineffable brilliance to their work on stage. We worked hard but with great joy, much laughter and a strong sense of purpose each and every day. I encouraged everyone's belief in the validity of our concept with the historical research that I had gathered and by frequently reminding myself and this colorful cast that some of Mr. Porter's favorite interpreters of his great songs were African American performers, including Ella Fitzgerald, Nat King Cole, Bricktop, Lena Horne and the great Bobby Short. I choose to think that dear Cole was looking down on us from Composer's Heaven, smiling happily at our efforts and turning to Noël Coward to say that our version of his masterpiece was "Wunderbar!" I believe that he also would have said that our Swingin' the Shrew was a truly joyful experience.

But offstage there were ever-less-joyful things going on....

In the musical *Promises, Promises* the ever-suffering mistress character assesses her situation at one point in the action, and she smartly sings about "knowing when to leave," "going while the going is good," and anticipating the time to "Fly!" That lyric frequently came into my head at some point, and I knew that the time was right to take her very good advice! Though I still was enthralled by the work with the artistic community and loving the opportunities that I could provide both for myself and for others in my beautiful artistic home, I knew that it

was time to fly! That gut instinct that I relied on so heavily in building the theater was telling me that all of the roads that had led me to The Playhouse were now well paved on the other side. It was time to choose a different direction and travel on.

It was not just instinct, however. It was a disconcerting and unsatisfying feeling that was brought on by a shift in the dynamics at the theater. Though not without occasional disagreements and spirited discussions, I had always enjoyed an overall good relationship with the board chairs and board members during my tenure. Even when I found them to be supportive but perhaps less active and dynamic than would have been my preference, I always felt that

My Petruchio and his Kate, Wayne Brady and Merle Dandridge, Pasadena Playhouse, 2014 (photograph by Jim Cox).

their hearts were in the right place. And most certainly they had been involved in a vital way during the intermission period. Most, if not all of them, stuck with it as we passed out of that darkness of the intermission and into the light once again. I was very grateful for their support during that challenging time and very happy that we were able to celebrate together as we not only started to actively resume producing but actually made those lights shine even more brightly.

At the same time, however, a number of circumstances brought a new energy to the board. A new board chair landed in that position because of an unfortunate accident which made Sheila Grether, one of our best board leaders incapacitated for a period of time and unable to continue in that role. The field in which this new board chair was accomplished was the banking industry. As a result he was very good with numbers and finances in a way that I suspect served him well in that line of work but had little or nothing to do with the customary operations and certainly not the philosophy of running an arts organization. The fact that his banking establishment was a generous supporter of the arts and other community services was certainly a plus, and this bank had indeed been generous to the theater. But, as well we know, "power corrupts and absolute power corrupts absolutely." That was certainly true in this case.

While I was most certainly willing, in fact eager, to share whatever power had rightly come my way after 18 years of service to the organization and a lifetime of experience in the field, I was certainly not willing to relinquish my place in what should be a partnership to someone who had no understanding of how to run a theater. I always believed that an artistic director should work *with* the board chair, not *for* the board chair. And the time came when I had to make that philosophy clear.

If I had suffered before from the pressure to be a hitmaker, that flame was turned way up by this individual, who felt that every project for the theater should be chosen to be critic proof, failure proof and guaranteed for success even if that meant that it had no artistic reason to exist or aesthetic viability. When I told him that this was both impossible and undesirable for me personally, he challenged me by saying, "Well, why not? Isn't that what they do on Broadway?" thus pretty much proving that he had no understanding of that sector of the business either. I had to firmly let him know that the ratio of hits to failure in the commercial theater was very low. And further, that many of those things that achieved the greatest success on Broadway were those productions that were arguably the most risky, the most brave, the most unexpected and most decidedly not the things that were run through some cookie-cutter process to make them commercially successful. Though true, I suspect that he did not believe me.

This argument went on far too long and far too often. Finally, I had to let him know, rather directly I am sure, that I would never be so brazen as to tell him how to run his business (though given some unfortunate events that emerged at his institution shortly after this time, perhaps I should have), so I would kindly request that he not assume that he should tell me how to run mine. As you can imagine, this did not pull us further into a relationship that would be described as warm and fuzzy. And that was quite all right with me!

While he backed off from looking over my shoulder quite so directly, he continued odious and disruptive whispers to other board members behind my back. Wisely, most of them did not give his comments much weight or credence but sadly some did, which made for some suddenly unexpected and uncomfortable comments at board meetings unlike anything that I had previously experienced. Needless to say, this took a good deal of the joy out of the job. I believe that it is not a job that I or anyone should do without a great quotient of joy, and, though never joyless, the joy quotient was diminishing.

My difficult relationship with that board chair alone was something that I could have handled. But the challenges did not come from him solely as there was something else that proved extremely challenging around this time. It was a not-so-subtle and very perceptible shift in the feel of my theater and of theaters all over the country. In conversations with my colleagues, fellow artistic and managing directors I learned that they also were feeling the ever-growing pressure to treat their companies like a business and not like an arts institution. This was an unfortunate trend in our field both then and now. I certainly understood that theaters needed to have strong business practices, though profit and loss should not be at the center of the mission, nor the first and only priority. They are called "not-for-profit" companies for many very good reasons. This shift in the way of thinking about the theater amplified and agitated my instinctive feelings that it was time to fly. This meant giving up the abundant comforts of having a wonderful artistic home and parting with the still great satisfaction that came from being at the center of a much-cherished artistic community. The thought of that was painful and heart tugging. But the time had come to be what I would later refer to as "unburdened" and unshackled from some of the more overwhelming and far-less-enjoyable tasks that come with the job. Also, quite frankly, I realized that I was involved in some of the same disagreements and discussions about the value of art over commerce and the importance of what we do over and over again. I was experiencing far too much déjà vu during these moments, to the point where that sometimes overwhelmed the ongoing satisfactions of the artistic process and the great rewards of collaborating with the artists. Time to "Fly!"

That is why I announced my intention to depart a good two years ahead of my planned exit at the end of the 2016–17 season, which would mark two decades in the job. I knew that it was important to get the word out there well ahead of time before any other event, good or bad, would make it imperative for me to stay on. This time I was really making that exit stage right, walking into the wings and out of my beloved theater.

The announcement of my departure was surprisingly front page news in the august *LA Times*. Actually, the story was teased on the front page and printed on page one of the Entertainment section. But still, pretty surprising and impressive I would say. The news was greeted with as vast an array of reactions as the announcement of my walking into the job had been two decades before. Good times and bum times, I always felt that it was vital to maintain a brave public face no matter what was going on. As a result there were very few people who knew about any unhappiness on my part beyond that tenacious fundraiser Lesley, who had now become my lovely wife, and a few very close friends. So, the primary reaction was shock mixed with sadness, especially in the artistic community. Very few people actually choose to walk away from such a good job of their own choice.

In truth, harkening back to my earliest days, there were some who clicked their heels with joy as this meant that they could finally get "their" theater back! Somehow against the odds this kid from Compton had managed to hang in there and, from their point of view, keep the theater in the grip of his "Black agenda" for all of this time. Despite ugly and consistent efforts by some, I had never been forced out or chased away. But now, those evil forces had an opportunity at long last. Perhaps, from their sad and misguided point of view, this meant that the "dark era" was finally over and that things could get back to where they should be. Surely those in charge would not make the same mistake and foolishly hire another person of color to replace me—surely that would not happen.

And indeed that did not happen—my successor was a lovely and kind young man with passion, theatrical savvy and motivation, but he was definitely not of a darker hue. There were whispers from some that this hire represented "The Great White Hope" who would bring back their nice, comfortable, cozy and colorless theater, which was just as they wanted it! Much to his credit, Danny Feldman did not. He made many admirable steps in the name of diversity in a number of areas on his own and has faced the challenges of running the theater admirably.

This sentiment was rarely spoken out loud, but it was spoken, and not always quietly. Most certainly it was in the subtext of many a reaction that came my way. I am fairly sure that ultimately pushing the theater away from its focus on diversity and inclusion was very much the aim of some on the board, and that meant getting the place out of my clutches. In truth, I held on for as long as I did so that those who sadly felt this way became the victims of their own sad delusions. No one had run me out of town on that rail. I rode away proudly because I was ready to move on. I was not pushed out; I exited gracefully with my head held proudly high.

Overall the reactions that I got from all over the country were kind, loving, supportive, understanding and most of all grateful and appreciative. So many expressed their understanding of how much Pasadena Playhouse had changed and evolved during my tenure. They genuinely and avowedly recognized that in so many ways it was a far different and far greater theater as a result of my time there. It had become a theater that was now deserving of respect, recognition and a return to a rightful place of honor in American theater history. So many articulated what I knew in my heart, that I had made a difference and changed a place for the better. That was and is truly gratifying.

Packing up my office at the theater was like a very long emotional walk down memory lane. I had held on to so many things that I had not looked at for years. Old programs, newspaper articles, photographs, correspondence and letters from friends and colleagues. It was both invigorating and sometimes painful to go through all of this and force myself to part with so many physical manifestations of my life in this theater. Going through all of this made me realize how very much I would miss being in the artistic community that I had worked so hard to create at The Playhouse. I was always so happy to know that we treated the artists well and that most of them were eager to return to work with us again or for frequent celebrations on opening nights or to support us with fundraising events. I often described working at the theater as being akin to having a house with a great kitchen. It was nice not to have to cook ALL of those great meals. Especially the ones that did not come out perfectly, but the process is what was always to be admired and respected. I had come to love opening up this great space for others to come in individually and collectively to show off their "culinary" skills by making a new work for our stage.

I felt blessed to share this great space with so many artists that I admired and cherished. Giving that up would be hard, and I would miss that.

What I would not miss was having some of the same conversations with the board over and over again as I pushed, prodded and cajoled them into a greater sense of ambition for the theater. Even after so many seasons I still found myself answering some of the most basic questions about what it meant to be a great arts organization and what was needed in terms of ongoing support to make that happen. I was weary of proclaiming yet another time that the arts are vital to the health of our society and as healing and evolving as a great university or a well-run hospital. I believed it passionately as much as I ever did, but proclaiming it over and over again had become enervating. I knew in my heart that it was getting harder and harder to "light myself on fire" in service to the theater. That task is truly noble, but I was honestly ready to pass that torch on to someone else. That too told me strongly that it was time to go.

Not only was cleaning out my office a time of purging and rediscovery; it was also a time for reflection. Even before I moved into that office and certainly during my very first weeks there I remember thinking that I would do this for four or five years, and that would be good. But five became ten somehow, and then ten miraculously became 20. As I closed up the final boxes and took down the last few posters that brought back such great memories, I found myself asking the same question that ran through my mind decades earlier, "How did that happen?"

Though I have tried many times, I can't really answer that question. And, once again, how it happened is far less important than that it did happen. I committed myself to a job and dedicated myself to a place and to a mission, and I made many great things happen with the help and support of so many. WE did that. WE made it happen. I said in an interview shortly before my departure that building this theater was the great work of my life, which had been full of many opportunities to do a lot of great work all over the world. I have been blessed to fulfill so many, if not indeed all, of the desires that I had early in my career. That is quite a statement. But I knew then as I know now that this is the truth. During those wonderful 20 years I gave and I took some of the very best of my directions. And that made quite a difference. That's a wonderful thing to feel and to know. I made a difference.

Epilogue: Back
on the Road(s) Again

It really is true that I have always believed in taking "The Leap of Faith." I firmly believe in closing one door to allow other doors to open. I believe in it, I have done it, and it has paid off. But it is still a frightening thing to do. Jumping off of that cliff with the hope of soaring, but knowing that a quick fall is also possible is chill making no matter how brave one pretends to be. But as John F. Kennedy once said, "Only those who dare to fail greatly can ever achieve greatly." So that great leap is often needed and sometimes demanded.

My firm decision to leave Pasadena Playhouse was the right choice, but in truth I made that choice not knowing what, if anything, would follow. Blessedly, the time between making that decision and this very moment has been full and rewarding. But that knowledge was to come over the years post departure; it was not within me in the days when I took my leap off of that metaphorical cliff. Gratefully, opportunities did come knocking in a rewarding way very quickly.

Shortly before my last months at the theater, I was invited to Houston to speak to the board of directors of a major musical theater company called Theatre Under the Stars. It was started decades earlier as an outdoor theater and earned that name from performing under the constellations in various parks in the city. At the time that they reached out to me the company was producing in the beautiful but humongous Hobby Center in the downtown Theatre District, not far from an old theatrical friend of mine the Alley Theatre. Built to live up to Texas standards, the huge auditorium is dazzling and enormous and inspired by this resident theater company; it literally has stars in the ceiling overhead. One can look up, hopefully before and after the acts and not during, and see the Universe sparkling in what appears to be a celestial shower of stars. Pretty stiff competition for whatever

Receiving the Alumni Achievement Award at Carnegie Mellon University, 2019.

is happening down on the stage. But as always a theater has its challenges!

The company had gone through a rough few years with a number of recent changes in their senior leadership. I was asked to speak to the board about focusing their efforts, putting things back on track and moving forward with the confidence that the company deserved after more than 50 years in business. But that confidence had been badly shaken by staff changes, some legal issues, and a less-than-stellar artistic reputation. I guess that I spoke pretty damn well, because at the end of that meeting I was asked by the executive committee if I would be interested in taking charge of the company. Flattering but certainly unexpected and a bit overwhelming. I politely declined the generous offer, primarily because I had several months left to go at Pasadena Playhouse. Flattery, of course, is seductive, and Texans do know how to flatter. So I accepted a position as their artistic advisor with the hope that I could help them right the ship and send it sailing into a brighter future. I spent the next year commuting between Southern California and Houston on a regular basis in an effort to do just that.

As I had done previously in Pasadena, I put the focus squarely on two things—artistic excellence and diversity of programming. The theater had fallen into an unhealthy cycle of remounting productions that had been done before, often sloppily and without real focus on the artistry involved. It was in the sad state of just producing something rather than producing something with an eye towards excellence. That had to change! Also, in a very large and dynamic city that was already one of the most ethnically diverse urban centers in the country, the theater onstage, backstage, in the offices and in the audiences was a sea of whiteness. That also had to change! And quickly!

Taking a smaller but equally adventurous leap of faith I convinced everyone that the upcoming season had to be rethought and redesigned. Rather than yet another season of yet another six shows with all-white or nearly all-white companies, I suggested a season that would truly reflect the rich diversity of the city in a much-more-dynamic way. This was scary, bold and some might say foolhardy (and in fact some did say that). But the announcement of the change was greeted with real enthusiasm by the press, the artistic community and eventually by most of the ticket buyers, including the vitally important new audiences who came to see themselves reflected on this glorious stage, perhaps for one of the first times. There was definitely a sense that TUTS was back, and back in a way that prompted the valuable phrase that I'd heard before, "Attention must be paid."

And attention was paid. Not just because the work of the theater was different but because it was also better, thanks to a staff which jumped on board with me, and a talented group of artists who gratefully accepted my invitation to come and work at the theater. It's so good to have friends and colleagues who will answer the call when you need them. Suddenly it was clear that the theater was not just rolling out yet another tired production. The work on stage now was new, vital and vigorous with an aim towards artistic excellence, hopefully at every level. This is not always achievable given the resources at hand in any situation. But it is the daring to aim high that counts. We dared to make our aim lofty, and sometimes we came very close to reaching the overhead stars. The season was received with critical praise, increased sales and new enthusiasm from all involved.

After many months in this advisory capacity, I was asked again to stay on and commit to being the company's artistic director, and a generous multiyear contract was proffered. Though certainly attractive and seductive, I knew that I was not ready to jump back into that position right away even with all of the enticements that were being offered by the company, the city, and the work itself. Having recently "unburdened" myself of the rewarding but frequently overwhelming necessities of running a company, I certainly was not eager to place that heavy backpack on my shoulders once again. I respectfully declined their generous offer and helped to guide them in their search for new leadership who would be prepared to make a long-term commitment that would build on the work that we had done together during my time there. I am happy to say that this was accomplished, and the company continues to thrive.

I seemed to be getting good at this closing of doors. Perhaps too good for my own good, I sometimes worried. As there were still moments when I wasn't quite sure what was next ... if anything at all. To continue the door analogy just a bit longer, fortunately mine was knocked on fairly quickly and quite often.

I spent the next several years back on various roads following the freelance directing path, directing a number of projects new and old on both coasts and in between. As I had for many years, I also subsidized my "theater habit" with a fair amount of work directing episodic television.

One of the first of these freelance gigs ironically brought me back to the show that really got me going so many decades ago at The Production Company and then beyond. I had a meeting with Paul Crewes, the artistic director of the recently opened Wallis Annenberg Performing Arts Center in Beverly Hills. In discussing other projects Paul suddenly asked, "Didn't you create *Blues in the Night*?" It turned out that Paul had produced the show during his days in Great Britain at one of the major regional theaters in that country. He asked if I might consider revisiting the show in the smaller black box theater at The Wallis. When we went downstairs to take a look, I was floored by how much this dynamic space was like the Donmar Warehouse in London, where the show had been so successful and launched the long run on the West End. Though I had made a silent, personal vow to leave the direction of the show to others many years earlier, I was too overcome with the theatrical romance of this situation to say no. There was just something too right about doing the show in this intimate space, in a beautiful new performing arts center in my hometown with actors that I knew would be available from previous productions during my many years of producing in Pasadena. I don't believe that I jumped at the opportunity, but I did allow myself to be pulled in without too much tugging.

I am so glad that I did. I had a wonderful cast and creative team, and the rehearsal period was joyful and productive. Though I walked into the process assuming that I knew everything about directing this particular very personal project, it was delightful and delicious to discover that because I knew more, I had much more to offer now. There was gold to be mined if I put my all-too-knowing self to the side and approached it as I would any new musical. I could actually make it better because—surprise, surprise—I was better, and I had more to give, even to this piece that I knew like the back of my well-worn hand. I took many of my old directions but also threw many out and found new ones that enhanced, heightened and re-energized the material. The result was a production that was greeted on opening night with the same jolt of dynamic excitement that could be felt in the room on that first night at The Production Company and several years later on opening night at the Donmar. What a rare and wonderful experience it was to have my past come crashing so thrillingly into my present and to know clearly that I had actually learned a thing or two during the in-between years. The kid from Compton was pretty lucky to have such a rare and supernal experience.

The post-Pasadena Playhouse years were full and busy. At least for a while. Then the whole world including the world of the theater was struck by a series of events that brought things to a screeching halt and put the brakes on everything in 2020. Shortly after that world-stalling pandemic, the entire nation and the American Theatre were thrust into action by a tragic event that could not be ignored given the horrifying visual evidence of wrongdoing that was put before our eyes. The nation was pushed into much-needed conversations of a very deep nature about our "National Health" on all levels. And within the theater field I found myself once again "Chased by Race" as my presence was requested and sometimes demanded for conversations which drastically changed our field very quickly in ways that I hope will be long lasting and sustained.

I suspect you know by now that I am talking about the Covid-19 pandemic which rocked the world and shut down live performances everywhere. The pandemic gave new meaning to the phrase that I once uttered onstage in that production of "Julius Caesar" so many years ago. Beware the Ides of March indeed! For it was in the middle of March of that year that Broadway, performing arts companies and regional theaters all over the country played their last performances for a projected period of two weeks to a month that turned into a much longer intermission lasting more than a year and a half. Beyond that, it was during this period of isolation and medical terror that another event of nearly Shakespearean proportions took place with the tragedy of George Floyd, who was brutally and torturously murdered in Minneapolis, a horrifying tragedy that rocked the world. The declarations that Black Lives Matter and the cries for racial justice were heard around the globe.

The shouting was not at all lost on the world of the theater. The horrible event in Minneapolis and the protests and marches that followed very quickly ignited the theater field as well. More fuel was almost literally poured onto this fire with the emergence of an exhaustive document called, "We See You White American Theatre" that was signed by many of the most well-known and highly respected artists of color in our field and further supported by hundreds of others. A theater industry that had already been rocked by the pandemic now found itself in an even greater volcanic event brought about by the cries for racial justice in every area of our society, but particularly in the world of the theater.

The shock that was felt throughout the entertainment industry was real and profound. Despite the fact that these issues had been discussed for many years, even decades, the issues of racism and discrimination in the theater were a dirty little

Blues in the Night at the Wallis Annenberg Center, Los Angeles, 2018.

secret that few were courageous enough to fully acknowledge. Even worse, those working in the field did an awful lot of self back patting as they declared themselves to be above this fray and free of any racial issues that needed to be faced. The events of that year took the hands that were patting the backs, and those hands slapped the American Theatre in the face. Once the shock was over, there were many voices that said you better stop fooling yourselves and face your own complicity in the overall still extant systemic racism in America and in the American Theatre, and you'd better face that right NOW!

It must be said that the theater field did indeed take up that responsibility, and suddenly the disturbingly calm and quiet days brought on by the pandemic were over and we were thrust into action again. Those quiet days were quite quickly filled with Zoom meetings, conference calls, webinars, podcasts and private conversations intended to address these vitally important issues. Not surprisingly, as one who had raised his voice frequently and loudly over the years about both the overt and covert racism in our field and the need to truly diversify our American theaters, I was drawn into these conversations, meetings and conference calls on a frequent and for a while near-constant basis.

Quite honestly, I found myself dealing with a number of emotional responses to this call. Frankly, I was weary of having this conversation ... once again! I was angry and frustrated that these issues were being addressed as if they were new when in fact they had been the subject of ongoing discussions and meetings at theater gatherings over far-too-many years with little and certainly not enough real change and action. I felt the deep lethargy that comes from feeling drawn into a fight that I had been fighting with varying degrees of success, but always with resentment, for far too long. But I came to see quite clearly that there did seem to be something different this time.

First and foremost, there were many more voices being raised now. Time had brought about the welcome hiring of far more people of color in leadership positions at major theaters, so I was not fighting the battle with too small a cadre of fellow fighters. That alone gave our voices strength, courage and volume which was undeniable and not to be ignored. I believe that the collision of events over that summer made it not just possible but necessary to face these controversial topics with greater honesty, with more focused time and with a greater intent to actually take words into action. "The fire this time" was burning with a far greater intensity and a much stronger need for it to be extinguished than ever before. Given all of that, I once again found strength and a renewed energy. I found the resources to give new vitality to a voice that had grown weary from shouting, to raise a fist at the top of a tired arm, and to gaze intently back into eyes that wanted mine to blink in fear or submission. I did not and we did not during this time. The strength in numbers gave each individual voice greater volume, and in our combined voices we found new levels of passion for the cause, tenacity and strong intent in our bonding. White American Theater did indeed see us, and they did hear us! The voices were so strong that they had to! Commitments and vows of change were made over several months of that year, and there were many immediate actions taken at theaters of all sizes, both commercial and institutional, that augured real change and dynamic differences going forward.

Only time will tell if these commitments will be sustained and if the actions that came out of the tsunami of words spoken will be as healing as they need to be and if the promised changes will be sustained. I do hope so. In truth, our lives in the theater are often driven by that one elusive-but-ever-so-powerful necessity: Hope.

Walking by faith (either religious, spiritual or artistic) and not by sight is a regular and necessary exercise for a life in the arts. Hope is a constant companion. I hope this idea is worth going forward. I hope this turns out well. I hope this work will have an audience. I hope that my audience recognizes my intentions and is willing to go along for the ride. I've learned to live in and with hope throughout my life. So I do hope that the American Theatre will take the lessons of that long, hot summer to heart and move towards a truly more equitable institution free of racism and discrimination, which allows all of its artists equal opportunity and equal access. Is that hoping for too much? I don't think so. I hope not.

Over many years I believe that I have opened some doors along the way to help make this a reality. I am told that I have. I have certainly tried. There are some strong examples now that substantiate the reality that the change is real. I am pleased and proud of the fact that none of the current leaders of color of major theaters around the country have to think of themselves as "The One." They are now a strong and mighty band. Also, a new crop of BIPOC associate artistic directors, resident artists, and others in leadership positions at theaters large and small are serving their institutions well now and preparing themselves to be the leaders of the future. Over several months I hosted a podcast series of conversations with all of these brilliant young leaders that was sponsored by the SDC Foundation, a truly valuable organization that nurtures and supports directors and choreographers at all stages of their careers. Those conversations have been valuable for those involved and for the many who have listened. That too is a blessing.

All of this progress has made being "Chased by Race" well worth the time, effort and the occasional pain that I have experienced. Pushing those doors open has not been easy, but it has been worth it. I am so very proud of all of those who have come rushing through to blaze their own trails and create their own new directions. They will open the next set of doors. All of this means that this Black Life has Mattered. This Black Life Still Matters.

I also am still pushing through new doors. In the fall of that tempestuous year I was invited to take on an artistic leadership position at the historic and venerable Ford's Theatre in Washington, DC. In that beautiful theater, with the spirit of Abraham Lincoln always looming in that infamous box just above stage left, as the theater's senior artistic advisor I dedicated myself once again to helping a theater company to further its diversity initiatives, reach out to new audiences and sustain a strong history of artistic excellence. I am blessed to have that opportunity once more and excited about the work that we have already done and all that we will do going forward.

Isn't that what it is all about? Going forward. Always pushing ahead, using all of the knowledge that one has hopefully gained over the years of a life in the theater to answer new questions, explore new territory. To be brave enough to walk into different rooms rather than revisiting old ones and repeating what you've done before. Going forward. Asking, what's next? What's around that very dark or very well-lit corner? Where can I go on the next leg of this journey? Those questions are all good and important ones. And once again, I constantly hope to find more and better answers one of these days.

As always and as ever, those answers will come from doing, not from thinking about the questions. So, though I am just a kid from Compton, I will keep doing. I will keep going forward. I will hear the words of my father and keep "Holding on!" Hope, determination, tenacity, a little Southern Arrogance, a good reputation and certainly a bit of luck give me the great luxury of knowing that there are indeed other journeys still ahead of me and other doors to open.

Time to get back on the road.

Time to keep traveling in my own directions.

Index

Numbers in **bold italics** indicate pages with illustrations

185

Index

Index

Index